Volatility Surface and Term Structure

Volatility Surface and Term Structure provides different financial models, based on options to predict underlying asset prices and design the risk-hedging strategies. Authors of the book have made theoretical innovations to these models to enable the models to be applicable to the real market. The book also introduces risk management and hedging strategies based on different criteria. These strategies provide practical guides for real option trading.

This book studies the classical stochastic volatility and deterministic volatility models. For the former, the classical Heston model is integrated with volatility term structure; the correlation of the Heston model is considered to be variable. For the latter, the local volatility model is improved from the experience of financial practice; the improved local volatility surface is then used for price forecasting. VaR (Value at Risk) and CVaR (Conditional Value at Risk) are employed as standard criteria for risk management. The options trading strategies are also designed to combine different types of options, and they have proved to be profitable in the real market.

This book is a combination of theory and practice. Users will find the applications of these financial models in the real market to be effective and efficient.

Shifei Zhou received his Master's degree in Computer Science and Technology from Central South University in Changsha, China. He is currently pursuing a PhD in the Department of Management Sciences at the City University of Hong Kong. His research interests mainly focus on financial behavior, derivatives, and risk management.

Hao Wang received his Bachelor's degree in Computer Science and Technology from Northwestern Poly-technical University in Xi'an, China. He is currently pursuing a PhD in the Department of Management Sciences at the City University of Hong Kong. His research interests mainly focus on risk management, financial derivatives, and financial engineering.

Kin Keung Lai received his PhD at Michigan State University, USA, in 1977 and is currently a Chair Professor of Management Science at the City University of Hong Kong. He is the President of the Asia-Pacific Industrial Engineering and Management Society, the General Secretary of the Hong Kong Operational Research Society, and a council member of the International Federation of Operations Research Societies. His main research interests include supply chain and operation management, forecasting, computational intelligence, and risk analysis.

Jerome Yen received his PhD at the University of Arizona, USA, in Systems Engineering and Management Information Systems. He is now a Professor of Accounting and Finance at Tung Wah College. Prior to his current post, he was a senior member of the Academic Advisory Committee, PRMIA, President of the Asia Pacific Association of Financial Engineering, and Co-Chair of the First Asia Pacific Conference on Financial Engineering held in Hong Kong in 2008. His main research interests include financial engineering, investment management, market and credit risk management, financial product development, trading strategies, and hedge funds.

I0894656

Routledge Advances in Risk Management

Edited by Kin Keung Lai and Shouyang Wang

Volatility Surface and Term Structure
High-profit options trading strategies
Shifei Zhou, Hao Wang, Kin Keung Lai and Jerome Yen

Volatility Surface and Term Structure

High-profit options trading strategies

**Shifei Zhou, Hao Wang,
Kin Keung Lai and Jerome Yen**

Routledge
Taylor & Francis Group
LONDON AND NEW YORK

First published 2013
by Routledge
4 Park Square, Milton Park, Abingdon, Oxon OX14 4RN
605 Third Avenue, New York, NY 10017

First issued in paperback 2017

Routledge is an imprint of the Taylor & Francis Group, an informa business

British Library Cataloguing in Publication Data
A catalogue record for this book is available from the British Library

Library of Congress Cataloging in Publication Data
Zhou, Shifei.
Volatility surface and term structure: high-profit options trading strategies/
Shifei Zhou, Hao Wang, Kin Keung Lai and Jerome Yen.
p. cm. – (Routledge advances in risk management; 1)
Includes bibliographical references and index.
1. Stock options. 2. Options (Finance). 3. Investments.
4. Speculation.
I. Title.
HG6042.Z466 2013
332.64'53–dc23 2013002738

ISBN 13: 978-1-138-91626-5 (pbk)
ISBN 13: 978-0-415-82620-4 (hbk)

Typeset in Times New Roman
by Sunrise Setting Ltd, Paignton, UK

Contents

List of figures vii
List of tables viii
Preface ix

1 Introduction 1

1.1 Implied volatility 2
1.2 Local volatility model 4
1.3 Stochastic volatility model 4

2 A novel model-free term structure for stock prediction 6

2.1 Introduction 6
2.2 Volatility model 7
2.3 Model-free term structure 7
2.4 Empirical tests 10
2.5 Conclusions 15

3 An adaptive correlation Heston model for stock prediction 16

3.1 Introduction 16
3.2 Adaptive correlation coefficient model 18
3.3 Empirical tests 21
3.4 Conclusions 23

4 The algorithm to control risk using options 25

4.1 Introduction 25
4.2 Theoretical background and model 26
4.3 Discussion 30
4.4 Conclusions 31

5 Option strategies: evaluation criteria and optimization 32

5.1 Introduction 32
5.2 Theoretical background and model 34
5.3 Results 38
5.4 Conclusions 39

6 A novel mean reversion-based local volatility model 41

6.1 Introduction 41
6.2 Motivations 42
6.3 Mean reversion-based local volatility model 42
6.4 Local volatility surface 46
6.5 Empirical tests 47
6.6 Conclusions 50

7 Regression-based correlation modeling for the Heston model 51

7.1 Introduction 51
7.2 The Heston model 52
7.3 Regression-based correlation coefficient 52
7.4 Empirical tests 54
7.5 Conclusions 57

8 Index option strategies: comparison and self-risk management 58

8.1 Introduction 58
8.2 Review 59
8.3 Theoretical background and model 61
8.4 Results and analysis 62
8.5 Conclusions 67

9 Call–put term structure spread-based Hang Seng Index analysis 71

9.1 Introduction 71
9.2 Theoretical background and model 73
9.3 Results and analysis 78
9.4 Conclusions 81

Notes 82
References 83
Index 86

Figures

2.1 Model-free term structure fitting curve 12
2.2 Heston and CEV IV process 13
2.3 Heston and CEV HSI process vs HSI 14
3.1 Time series of the VHSI and the HSI 17
3.2 CEV implied volatility vs Heston implied volatility 23
5.1 Result of Monte Carlo simulation 38
6.1 Local volatility surface 43
6.2 Volatility surface by traditional local volatility model 48
6.3 Volatility surface by mean-reversion local volatility model 49
8.1 The mean value of Monte Carlo simulation 63
8.2 The mean expected return of these 16 strategies 64
8.3 The variance of expected return of these 16 strategies 65
8.4 The VaR of these 16 strategies 66
8.5 The variance of VaR of these 16 strategies 67
9.1 The implied volatility of 3 April 2012, 16:14 75
9.2 The implied volatility of 3 April 2012, 10:29 76
9.3 The implied volatility of 3 April 2012, 16:14 and 3 April 2012, 10:29 77
9.4 The HSI, IVP, and IVC 79
9.5 The HSI and DIF 80

Tables

2.1 One-day ahead comparison 15
3.1 Correlation coefficients between the VHSI and HSI 18
3.2 One-day ahead comparison 23
5.1 Ranking of basic style by VaR 39
5.2 The result of using option strategies for arbitrage 39
6.1 Comparison of forecasting power 49
7.1 Coefficient comparison of regression models 56
7.2 Prediction performance comparison of regression models 56
8.1 Mean value of expected return, VaR, CVaR, and the variance of these three criteria based on the Monte Carlo simulation from 12 December 2012 for the following 100 days 69
8.2 Mean value of expected return, VaR, CVaR, and the variance of these three criteria based on the Monte Carlo simulation from 12 February 2012 for the following 100 days 70
9.1 The results of the prediction 81

Preface

Options trading became popular from 26 June, 1973 when the Chicago Board Options Exchange (CBOE) standardized and integrated options contract transactions. Options expand the range of investment choices and help investors explore different investment channels. Generally, options can provide investors with good opportunities to obtain a higher income. There are many branches of research on options. The risk-hedge functionality of options is also welcomed by investors. Proper understanding and manipulation of the Greek risk indicators for options can help investors measure and manage risk.

This book proposes different financial models based on options prices to predict the underlying asset price and proposes designs for risk hedging strategies. The authors review the literature and improve traditional volatility models. Theoretical innovation is made for making these models suitable for real markets. Risk management and hedging strategies are designed and introduced based on different criteria. These strategies can provide practical guidance for real options trading based on results from theoretical models.

Half the chapters in this book focus on volatility models and the application of these models to market forecasting. The other half is oriented towards risk management and option trading strategies design.

Chapter 2 describes the use of an implied volatilities term structure-based Heston model to forecast the underlying asset price. The parameters of the Heston model are estimated by the least squares method. The term structure is calculated and applied to the Heston model as the long-run mean level. Finally, we simulate price distribution of the underlying assets on the basis of the Heston and constant elasticity of variance (CEV) models.

Chapter 3, motivated by the disadvantages of the traditional Heston model, proposes an adaptive correlation coefficient scheme to estimate Heston's parameters. To precisely estimate this correlation, the Heston model is trained by the least squares method on historical data every day when the underlying price is simulated based on the implied volatility term structure.

Chapter 4 describes the use of basic theories of option pricing and the method of simulation to clarify the significant role that options can play in risk management. The characteristics and hedging effects of options are analyzed by combining options with the underlying asset. This does not only widen the method of controlling risk but also promotes the development of options.

Chapter 5 describes the proposed way to manage risk in equity investments by applying VaR (Value at Risk) and CVaR (Conditional Value at Risk) as standard criteria. A model based on these criteria is built for the design of optimal strategies. Through empirical tests, we find that a good profit can be made when the prediction of the trend of the underlying asset price is highly efficient and precise. The loss is also effectively controlled even when the prediction is bad and inaccurate.

Chapter 6 studies the traditional local volatility model and proposes a novel one with a mean-reversion process. The more the local volatility departs from its mean level, the higher the rate at which local volatility reverts to the mean. Then, a Bi-cubic B-spline surface-fitting scheme is used to recover the local volatility surface. The Monte Carlo simulation is adopted to estimate the underlying asset price trend. Finally, empirical tests show our mean-reversion local volatility model has good predictive power compared with the traditional local volatility model.

In Chapter 7, we propose a regression-based dynamic correlation between the volatility and the underlying asset price which is estimated by three different regression models: simple, polynomial, and auto-regression. The prediction performance of these models is compared in empirical tests.

Chapter 8 describes options risk management by buying or selling the underlying assets to hedge potential risk, to a certain degree. We propose a self-risk management method to control risk. The combination of different types of options is designated self-risk management. The underlying asset price is predicted and used to back-test our self-risk management method.

In Chapter 9, we propose a novel call–put spread-based model for forecasting the price of the underlying asset. Curves of implied volatility of call and put options are calculated separately. The distance between the call and put implied volatility curves contains important market information. We use this distance to predict the underlying asset level and obtain a good result.

Shifei ZHOU
Department of Management Sciences
City University of Hong Kong
Kowloon, Hong Kong
Email: shifeizhou@gmail.com

Kin Keung LAI
Department of Management Sciences
City University of Hong Kong
Kowloon, Hong Kong
Email: mskklai@cityu.edu.hk

Hao WANG
Department of Management Sciences
City University of Hong Kong
Kowloon, Hong Kong
Email: haowang_2006@163.com

Jerome YEN
Department of Finance
Hong Kong University of
Science and Technology
Clear Water Bay, Hong Kong
Email: risksolution@gmail.com

December 28, 2012

1 Introduction

Stock options trading is a new way of stock trading developed in the 1970s, commonly used in the United States since the early 1990s. A stock option is a right to buy or sell a certain stock at a fixed price within a certain period of time. The buyer is not given the stock itself but the right to buy it at an agreed price.

Execution of an option in options trading is a process where the buyer decides whether to buy or sell the underlying asset at the price the seller and the buyer have agreed. The seller can only passively accept the compliance obligations. Once the buyer asks to execute the option contract, the seller must fulfill their obligations and settle the position specified in the option contract. Hence, the rights and obligations between the seller and the buyer are not equal. The underlying assets of options include commodities, stocks, stock index futures contracts, bonds, and foreign exchange.

The underlying asset of stock index options is the spot index. For example, in the case of the currently popular European option, buyers and sellers directly settle the option contract by cash for stock index options when these options expire. For real option trading, the buyer of a stock index option can only execute the buy right when the option generates the floating profit (earnings greater than the transaction fees) and foregoes the right when there is a loss (including the case where earnings are less than the transaction fee). Hence, there is less risk for the option buyer.

Stock index options sellers face the risk of loss only when they have to passively execute an option contract. However, as long as the premium that sellers collect from buyers can cover the losses, they can hedge the risk of losses. Based on volatility calculated from the stock index and stock index futures contracts, options sellers are able to control the risk of losses to a ninety-five percent confidence level by collecting a conservative premium rate of ten to fifteen percent.

Compared with commodity options, the execution of stock index options and stock index futures are two independent delivery processes. The underlying asset of stock index futures contracts is the spot price index. The stock index is usually composed of a basket of stocks. Commonly, the cash mode is used for settlement of stock index options. That is, the gains and losses of stock index investors are settled by cash at the maturity date of futures contracts.

The execution of stock index options is similar to stock index futures, which can be divided into two modes, US and European. Since the underlying asset of stock index options is also the spot stock index, stock index options are converted into stock index futures on the execution date (US mode) and are exercised with futures, such as the small Chicago Mercantile Exchange (CME) Standard & Poor's (S&P) 500 index futures and options. The European option is directly executed with cash at maturity, such as the CBOE S&P 500 Index options. However, for European options, the market price usually contains intrinsic value and time value. The intrinsic value is the expected value between the underlying asset price and the strike price at maturity. Hence, in this book, we make use of the market option price and do not discuss the intrinsic and time value of option prices in detail. The option price is also referred to as the market option price by default.

Options trading based on futures can provide a hedging function for the futures trader. To format a multi-level, especially low-risk high-yield portfolio in the futures market, you need to take advantage of options. To reduce the trading risk of futures investors, to expand the scope of market participants, and to improve market stability and liquidity also requires options. In addition, options can provide hedging tools for addressing risk in contractual agriculture and to protect farmers' revenue. The US government encouraged farmers to successfully combine their government subsidy with the options market so as to transmit the huge risks of the agricultural market to the futures market. This policy not only reduces the government's fiscal expenditure but also stabilizes agricultural production and effectively protects farmers' benefits.

In addition to hedging, stock index options also contain certain market information from participants. During the options trading process, buyers and sellers provide bid and ask prices for options. These prices contain views of buyers and sellers about what the underlying asset price is expected to be at the maturity date. Black and Scholes (1973) proposed that implied volatility, calculated from options prices, reflects market information. If the implied volatility of a put option is large, it means market participants are panicky about the future market trend. Conversely, if the implied volatility of a call option is large, this indicates that the market will go up in the near future. Therefore, the study of option implied volatility is significant and beneficial.

1.1 Implied volatility

The implied volatility of an option contract is volatility of price of the underlying asset which is implied in the price of the option. Implied volatility varies with different strikes and time to maturities. For a given time to maturity, the implied volatility varies with strikes; for a given strike, the implied volatility varies with different maturities. To price European options, Black and Scholes (1973) proposed that the price of underlying assets satisfies the following:

$$\frac{dS}{S} = \mu dt + \sigma dW$$

where μ is the mean value of historical price, σ is the constant variance of the underlying asset's price, and W represents a standard Wiener process. From Ito's

Lemma, the logarithmic of the underlying price should follow the formula:

$$d \ln S = \left(\mu - \frac{1}{2}\sigma^2\right)dt + \sigma dW$$

Therefore, the logarithmic of the underlying price follows a normal distribution. However, when applying this theory into practical market options, the normal distribution expresses the phenomenon of a fat tail at both sides of the distribution. Black and Scholes proposed this model based on the following assumptions: (1) no dividend before the option maturity; (2) no arbitrage; (3) a constant risk-free interest rate; (4) no transaction cost or taxes; (5) divisible securities; (6) continuous trading; and (7) constant volatility. For a given time during the trading day, if the market releases the option price, the option volatility can be calculated by inverting the Black–Scholes formula.

On the one hand, if the time to maturity is fixed, volatility smile is defined as a curve that the implied volatility changes with different strikes. In a long-observed pattern, the volatility smile looks like a smile. The implied volatility of an at-the-money option is smaller than that of in- or out-of-the-money options. When the implied volatility of an out-of-the-money put option is larger than that of an out-of-the-money call option, this curve is called implied volatility skew. Zhang and Xiang (2008) defined the concept of "moneyness" as the logarithm of the strike price over the forward price, normalized by standard deviation of expected asset return as follows:

$$\xi \equiv \frac{\ln(K/F_0)}{\overline{\sigma}\sqrt{\tau}}$$

where $\overline{\sigma}$ is the historical volatility of the underlying asset price; τ is the time to maturity; K is strike price; F is the forward index level. Then, implied volatility smirk is defined as employing the moneyness as an independent variable. Implied volatility changes according to moneyness.

On the other hand, if implied volatilities with different strikes and a given maturity are combined together under a certain weighted scheme, then the implied volatility term structure can be defined as a curve that implied volatilities change with different maturities. When the implied volatilities of call options and put options are calculated, we obtain a call implied volatility curve and a put implied volatility curve. The spread between call and put curve is called call–put term structure spread. This spread contains certain market information.

When implied volatility of put term structure is larger than that of call term structure, market participants worry about the market on the maturity date. If these two curves cross, there are two conditions. First, when implied volatility of the put curve is larger than call curve before the cross point and smaller after the cross point, it means the market trend may reverse in a short term and go up. Second, when implied volatility of call curve is larger than the put curve before the cross point and smaller after the cross point, it means the market trend may reverse in a short term and go down. Finally, when the implied volatility of call term structure is larger than that of put term structure, the view from investors is that the market still goes up. By using this functionality of term structure, we can employ the term structure to predict the underlying asset price efficiently, which is discussed in greater detail in Chapters 2 and 9.

1.2 Local volatility model

Local volatility also performs well in forecasting the underlying asset price. Local volatility is an instantaneous volatility that is a function of time t and underlying asset price S_t. Typically, Dupire (1994) presented a deterministic equation to calculate the local volatility from option price based on the assumption that all call options with different strikes and maturities should be priced in a consistent manner.

$$\sigma(K,T)=\sqrt{2\left(\frac{\frac{\partial C}{\partial T}+rK\frac{\partial C}{\partial K}}{K^2\frac{\partial^2 C}{\partial K^2}}\right)}$$

Nevertheless, this deterministic function suffers two weaknesses. First, because local volatility is a function of both strike and time to maturity and it is possible that not all strikes are available at each time to maturity, the number of local volatilities is finite and is usually not enough for further calculation and applications. As a result, researchers are inclined to use interpolation to obtain a series data of local volatility for further calculations. In this way, the algorithm of interpolation becomes very important because a weak algorithm results in problem of inadequate precision. Second, there is the intrinsic problem of the Dupire's equation. The indeterminancy of the equation may cause local volatility to be extremely large or very small. In Chapter 6, we propose a mean-reversion process to overcome these faults and improve the model. As local volatility is a function of time and underlying asset price, it has the ability of predicting the underlying asset price if we can construct the local volatility surface.

1.3 Stochastic volatility model

In the stochastic volatility model, volatility is considered as a stochastic process. The stochastic volatility model assumes that the underlying asset price follows a geometric Brownian process. In the Black–Scholes model, volatility is assumed to be constant over the time to maturity. However, this can explain the phenomenon that volatility smile and skew vary with different strikes. The stochastic volatility model can solve this problem. Typically, Heston (1993) proposed a model which considers the underlying asset price process and the volatility process as random processes. Moreover, these two processes have a constant correlation.

The underlying level process of Heston model is composed of two terms, the price drift term and the volatility with random motion term. The volatility process is also composed of two terms, a volatility drift with mean reversion functionality and a volatility of volatility with random motion. The model is formulated as follows:

$$dS_t = \mu(t)S_t dt + \sqrt{V_t}S_t dW_1$$
$$dV_t = \kappa(\theta - V_t)dt + \sigma\sqrt{V_t}dW_2$$

where θ is the long-run mean level of volatility, κ is the speed of instant volatility returning to long-run mean level, and σ is volatility of volatility. These three parameters satisfy the condition of $2\kappa_t\theta > \sigma^2$ and ensure the process of V_t is strictly positive. Furthermore, W_1 and W_2 are two standard Wiener processes and have a correlation of ρ.

The Heston model has been widely applied in equities, gold, and foreign exchange markets. Furthermore, many extended models based on the Heston model have been proposed. Christoffersen *et al.* (2006) proposed a two-factor stochastic volatility model based on the Heston model to control the level and slope of the volatility smirk. Andersen *et al.* (2002) and Chernov and Ghysels (2000) employed an Efficient Method of Moments approach to estimate structural parameters of the Heston model. Bates (2000) used an iterative two iterations procedure to measure the structural parameters and spot volatilities.

As the Heston model simulates the relationship between implied volatility and the underlying asset price, this model also has the ability of forecasting the underlying asset price. In Chapter 3, we use the Heston model to predict the Hang Seng Index (HSI) by considering the correlation of the underlying asset level and volatility process as dynamic variables. The underlying asset price is simulated by the analytic solution of geometric Brownian motion.

2 A novel model-free term structure for stock prediction

Implied volatility term structure contains market views. This chapter first calculates model-free implied volatility term structure and then applies it as the long-run mean level of Heston model. Since the Heston model assumes both underlying asset price process and volatility process as stochastic processes, the geometric Brownian motion is used to forecast the underlying asset price.

2.1 Introduction

2.1.1 Background

Volatility term structure represents that the implied volatility varies with different times to maturities. While analyzing implied volatility term structure, the key point is to figure out how the implied volatility is calculated from options market data. There are mainly two types of implied volatility valuation methods: the model-based implied volatility and the model-free implied volatility.

The most widely used model-based implied volatility valuation method is the Black–Scholes (BS) model. Researchers reverse the BS model and obtain a deterministic volatility function. However, this method suffers a number of constraints. Heston (1993) proposed a stochastic volatility model which assumes volatility is a stochastic process. Secondly, in the case of model-free volatility, Carr and Madan (1998), Demeterfi *et al.* (1999), Britten-Jones and Neuberger (2000) and Carr and Wu (2009) have presented a volatility expectation based on variance swap contracts. Britten-Jones and Neuberger (2000) further proposed an integrated volatility defined as the integral of call option price and put option price on all strikes at a given expiry date.

2.1.2 Motivation

Extant literature has showed that the BS model has a few shortcomings. First, for a given maturity, options with different strikes have different implied volatilities. This is the reason why the BS model can not explain the volatility smile curve. Second, it assumes implied volatility at a given maturity to be constant, which is unsuitable for predicting the underlying asset price trend. Hence, in this chapter, we prefer the model-free integrated implied volatility model but use a discrete form of the integral and consider the process risk-neutral.

Furthermore, the Heston model considers the process of change of the underlying asset's price as Geometrical Brownian movement with volatility as a stochastic process. We apply the Heston model, as well as the constant elasticity variance (CEV) model, to establish a deterministic relationship between the underlying price and volatility.

2.2 Volatility model

The Heston model is more complicated than the CEV model. It takes the mean-reversion term into consideration and the assumption is that the two processes of the underlying price and volatility are stochastic processes with a constant correlation to each other. The original Heston model is defined as follows:

$$\begin{aligned} dS_t &= \mu(t)S_t dt + \sqrt{V_t}S_t dW_1 \\ dV_t &= \kappa(\theta - V_t)dt + \sigma\sqrt{V_t}dW_2 \\ \rho &= \langle W_1, W_2 \rangle \end{aligned} \tag{2.1}$$

where θ is the long-run mean level of volatility, κ is the speed of instant volatility returning to long-run mean level, and σ is volatility of volatility. These three parameters satisfy the condition of $2\kappa_t\theta > \sigma^2$ and ensure the process of V_t to be strictly positive. Furthermore, W_1 and W_2 are two standard Wiener processes having correlation ρ.

2.3 Model-free term structure

2.3.1 Model-free implied volatility

Taylor *et al.* (2010) defined a model-free implied volatility which is an expected implied volatility obtained by integrating different option strikes by option prices. They compared this model-free implied volatility with at-the-money implied volatility and realized volatility in respect of volatility information content. They found that the model-free implied volatility outperforms the other volatility model and is more informative. Similarly, Carr and Wu (2009) defined a risk-neutral integrated volatility, marked as $E_t^Q[IV_{t,T}]$, over a given period $[t, T]$ through options with different strike prices.

$$E_t^Q[IV_{t,T}] = \frac{2}{T-t}\int_0^\infty \frac{Q_t(K,T)}{P_t(T)K^2}dK \tag{2.2}$$

where $P_t(T)$ is the value of a bond at time t, $Q_t(K,T)$ is the call option price at time t with strike price K, and maturity T when strike price K is greater than the underlying asset price or the put option price at time t with strike price K and maturity T when strike price K is less than the underlying asset price.

However, this is a continuum formula for model-free implied volatility. As we focus on the Hong Kong options market, we use a discrete version of Equation (2.2), as follows:

$$\sigma_t^2 = \frac{2}{T-t}\sum_i^N \frac{\Delta K_i}{K_i^2} e^{r(T-t)} Q_t(K,T) - \frac{1}{T-t}\left[\frac{F}{K_0} - 1\right]^2 \tag{2.3}$$

where N is the number of options for a given maturity T at time t, F is the forward price. According to the Hang Seng Index (HSI), forward price is defined as the forward index level of the HSI, calculated as follows:

$$F = K + e^{r(T-t)} \times (C_K - P_K) \tag{2.4}$$

where K is the strike price of out-of-the-money call or put options. C_K is the out-of-the-money call option price. P_K is the out-of-the-money put option price.

Since the model-free implied volatility is calculated on a given maturity with different strikes, we can draw an implied volatility term structure with different times to maturities, though for a given expiry, implied volatility is constant through the option lifetime. This is not really true in real markets. Therefore, we propose a cubic function to fit the implied volatility term structure. The spirit of the cubic function is similar to the least squares method.

We define the cubic function $\phi(x)$ as follows; the left hand side of the function represents the fitted implied volatility:

$$\phi(x) = a_0 + a_1 x + a_2 x^2 + a_3 x^3 = \sum_{i=0}^m a_i x^i \tag{2.5}$$

where $m = 3$ is the largest power of the variable, x represents time to maturity (measured in years). a denotes the corresponding parameters. Our aim is to find an optimal parameter vector a such that the difference between fitted implied volatility and real implied volatility is minimal. We define the difference δ_j to be the result of real data minus fitted data.

$$\delta_j = y_j - \phi_m(x_j) \tag{2.6}$$

where $j = 1, \ldots, n$, n means the total number of real implied volatility, y_j is the real implied volatility, and $\phi_m(x_j)$ is the estimated implied volatility at jth data point. It is hard to get an optimal vector only by comparing this difference because the difference may be small when the real data fluctuate dramatically through a constant mean value. Hence, we use a squared error method to compare the difference.

$$F(a_0, a_1, \ldots, a_m) = \sum_{j=1}^n \delta_j^2 = \sum_{j=1}^n [y_j - \varphi_m(x_j)]^2 \tag{2.7}$$

where $F(a_0, a_1, \ldots, a_m)$ represents the summation of fitting errors. Obviously, if we minimize the summation of errors, we will obtain an optimal parameter vector for the cubic function. Since the parabolic function will also have an optimal value at a given variable range, we differentiate (2.7) and get a partial differential equation of summation error function to a given parameter.

$$\frac{\partial F}{\partial a_i} = -2\sum_{j=1}^{n}\left[y_j - \sum_{i=0}^{m} a_i x_j^i\right] x_j^i = 0 \tag{2.8}$$

We let the partial differential result to be zero. In this way, the optimal value of the parabolic function is derived. By moving the real implied volatility to right hand side, (2.8) is transformed into (2.9).

$$\sum_{i=0}^{m} a_i \left(\sum_{j=1}^{n} x_j^{i+j}\right) = \sum_{i=1}^{n} y_j x_j^i \tag{2.9}$$

There are four parameters in the cubic function. Hence, $i = 0,\ 1,\ 2,\ 3$. At least four pairs of real data points are needed to compute the optimal parameter vector.

2.3.2 *Distribution of the price of the underlying asset*

By using the cubic parameter estimation, we can fit the curve of implied volatility term structure from real market data. In this section, this curve is used for stock price distribution analysis. But before we move on, it is necessary to return to the original Heston model, on which the stock price distribution is based.

By using historical options data, we are able to estimate the optimal parameters in the Heston model. Given these parameters, stochastic processes of the underlying asset price and volatility are derived from the Heston model. However, since the process of volatility is calculated from historical options data, which do not reflect the current or future market view of investors, the process of underlying price calculated by the volatility process also lacks future market information. Therefore, the implied volatility term structure described above is able to solve this problem because model-free term structure contains investors' expectations of the future options market. The process of volatility is generated from the Heston model by using the implied volatility term structure as the long run mean level. To take full advantage of implied volatility term structure, we generate the underlying price process, based on it.

In the basic Heston model, the underlying asset price is determined by a stochastic process with constant drift rate and stochastic volatility. Stochastic volatility is another stochastic process but has a correlation with the first process. Therefore, it is very similar to the geometric Brownian process (GBP). In GBP, the underlying asset price is a stochastic process with constant drift rate and constant volatility. Stochastic differential equation (SDE) of GBP is shown as follows:

$$dS_t = \mu S_t dt + \sigma S_t dW_t \tag{2.10}$$

where μ is the drift rate in percent. Basically, the drift rate is equal to the risk-free interest rate minus the stock dividend. σ is percent volatility. They are both assumed to be constant in the assumption of geometric Brownian movement. W_t is a standard Wiener process.

In our model, we have already fitted out the implied volatility term structure. The term structure of interest rate is also available from HIBOR.[1] For a given time t and initial stock price S_0, an analytical solution can be derived from the SDE of (2.10) by applying Ito's interpretation[2] (Ito, 1951).

$$S_{t+1} = S_t \exp\left(\left(\mu_t - \frac{V_t}{2}\right)t + \sqrt{V_t}W_t^S\right) \tag{2.11}$$

where S_t is the stock price at time t. Right hand side of (2.11) represents calculation of future stock price based on the initial value. For a given time t, the implied volatility is obtained from volatility term structure described above. μ_t is the drift rate, a function of time t. According to Steven Heston (1993), drift rate of the stochastic process is equal to the interest rate minus the stock dividend, namely, $\mu_t = r_t - D_t$. W_t^S is a Wiener process generated by normal distribution with mean of 0 and variance of 1. However, since W_t^S has an optimal correlation with W_t^V, they are calculated as follows:

$$\begin{aligned} W_t^V &= \sqrt{dt}\varepsilon \\ W_t^S &= \rho W_t^V + \sqrt{1-\rho^2}\sqrt{dt}\varepsilon \end{aligned} \tag{2.12}$$

Similarly, the stochastic process of implied volatility based on term structure is generated as follows:

$$V_{t+1} = V_t \exp\left[\left(\kappa(\theta - V_t) - \frac{\sigma^2}{2}\right)dt/V_t + \frac{\sigma W_t^V}{\sqrt{V_t}}\right] \tag{2.13}$$

where κ is the mean reversion speed; θ is the long run mean level of implied volatility obtained from the term structure; σ is volatility of volatility.

2.4 Empirical tests

2.4.1 CEV model

The CEV option price model was first proposed by Cox (1975), which contains the BS model. Cox assumes the underlying price process to be stochastic, driven by a differential equation.

$$dS_t = \mu S_t dt + \sigma S_t^\gamma dW_t \tag{2.14}$$

where μ, σ, and γ are constant parameters. μ is the drift rate. Here, we assume it to be risk-free interest rate. σ is volatility of volatility. γ is the constant parameter.

They satisfy conditions of $\sigma \geq 0$ and $\gamma \geq 0$. At any given time t, the standard deviation of returns is defined as follows:

$$V_t = \sigma S_t^{(\gamma-2)/2} \tag{2.15}$$

Therefore, the "CEV exponent" (Emanuel and MacBeth, 1982) γ determines the relationship between volatility and the underlying price. When γ equals to 2, volatility equals to the constant variable σ. This is the standard BS model and the option price in CEV model is the same as in the BS model. When γ is less than 2, we can see the leverage effect from (2.15), which means the underlying asset price increases when volatility decreases. In contrast, when γ is greater than 2, this is the so-called inverse leverage effect, where volatility rises with increase in the underlying price.

Based on the stochastic differential Equation (2.14), we can derive the distribution of the underlying price from stochastic volatility, as follows (according to geometric Brownian motion, GBM):

$$S_{t+1} = S_t \exp\left[\left(r_t - \frac{1}{2}\left(\frac{V_t}{S_t^{1-\gamma}}\right)^2\right)t + \frac{V_t\sqrt{t}W_t^S}{S_t^{1-\gamma}}\right] \tag{2.16}$$

where r_t is the risk-free interest rate.

In this section, we combine (2.15) and (2.16) and use the Monte Carlo simulation to calculate distribution of the underlying asset price. Given the initial underlying price S_0, we can calculate the initial volatility by applying (2.14). Iteratively, the next day price is computed from volatility of the previous day, by using (2.16).

2.4.2 *Empirical analysis*

2.4.2.1 *Data description*

For empirical tests, data are from HSI options. Although the original file contains transaction data of every minute, only the closing price of every day is treated as the option price. The options data spans from 2 January 2007 to 31 December 2009, covering 739 trading days and 321,932 trading records. Each record contains contract information of the option, trading time (precise to the second), bid and ask price at the trading time, risk-free interest rate, and closing price of the HSI. At the same time, we also compute simple averages of the bid and ask prices as the closing price of the option. Since the strike price and time to maturity are contained in the option contract, we can use the BS model to calculate the implied volatility from each entry data. To make the comparison convenient, we append the implied volatility at the end of each entry.

As implied volatility of options with different maturities and different strike prices can generate a surface, we calculate the implied volatility term structure from it by averaging the implied volatility along the strike axle. Furthermore as follows, we only consider options with maturities of less than six months. Figure 2.1 shows the average volatility over the next four months. The stars represent the implied volatility data before fitting. The solid line is the model-free term structure curve after fitting. This fitting curve functions as an average implied volatility for Heston model simulation. There are 21 trading days each month, so 21 points between each maturity.

2.4.2.2 *Heston and CEV simulation*

As mentioned in Section 2.4.1, the CEV model contains μ, σ, and γ constant parameters, in which μ is equal to the interest rate as we assume there are no dividends during the testing period. σ is volatility of volatility. Therefore, we calculate σ from the time series and consider σ as the standard deviation of the term structure. Then, there will be a unique sigma each day. According to Ncube (2009), the value of γ is important because γ determines the relationship between volatility and the underlying price. Similarly, we set γ equal to 0.5.

We estimate the parameters of Heston model using the historical market options data. The optimal parameters are set to be as follows:

$$\hat{\kappa} = 1.746, \quad \hat{\theta} = 0.306, \quad \hat{\sigma} = 0.499, \quad \hat{\rho} = -0.899$$

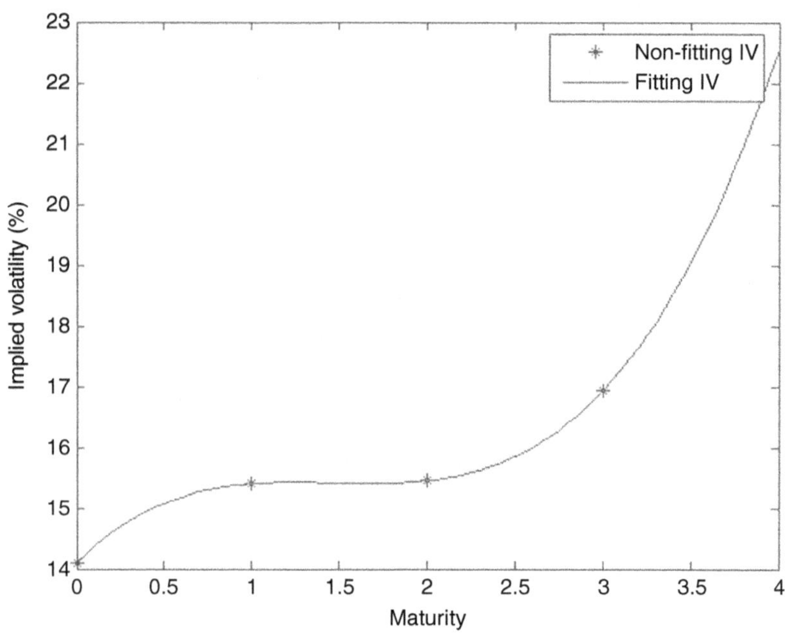

Figure 2.1 Model-free term structure fitting curve.

We simulate the Heston volatility process by using the term structure as the long-run mean level of volatility. The above optimal parameters are also used in simulation of the volatility process. When simulating the underlying price stochastic process, we fix the random seed of GBM solution to be 11. Then, the random motion term can be calculated from these random numbers. The random motion term of volatility process is calculated from that of the underlying asset price process by using the above correlation coefficient. Based on all these parameters, we generate the process as shown in Figure 2.2.

The solid line represents the mode-free fitting term structure. The star line is the stochastic process of CEV volatility. Due to the small value of γ, the volatility of volatility is small. The circled line is the Heston volatility process, generated by using the Monte Carlo simulation. After applying implied volatility term structure as long-run mean level, the volatility vibrates along the fitting term structure curve.

As described in Section 2.3.2, the underlying price process is also a stochastic process and has a correlation with the volatility process. The optimal correlation coefficient is -0.899. By using the result of Figure 2.2, we simulate the process of the underlying price as shown in Figure 2.3.

In Figure 2.3, the dotted line is the time series of the HSI from 2 December 2009 to 26 March 2010. The star line is the CEV underlying process of the HSI. The circled line is the Heston underlying process of the HSI. Since the process of underlying price has a high correlation with the volatility process, the underlying series also vibrates along the time series of the HSI.

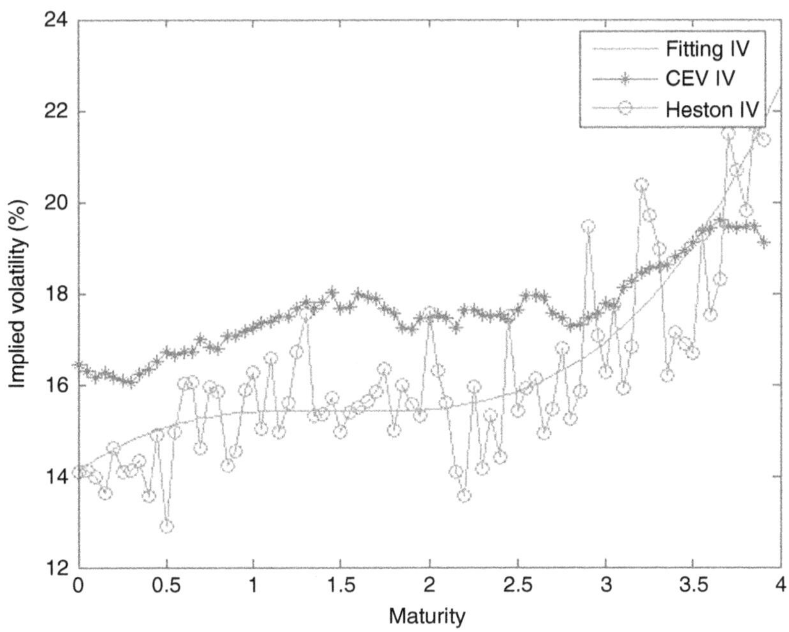

Figure 2.2 Heston and CEV IV process.

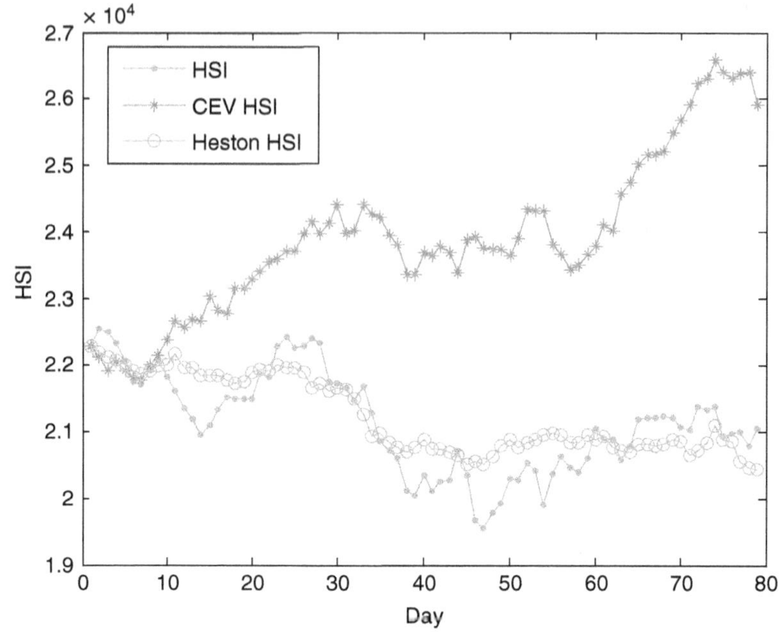

Figure 2.3 Heston and CEV HSI process vs HSI.

To evaluate the prediction ability, we compare the one-day-ahead prediction errors of CEV and Heston models. The error is measured by mean absolute error (MAE) in (2.17).

$$E = \frac{1}{N}\sum_{i=1}^{N} |\hat{y}_i - y_i| \tag{2.17}$$

where $\hat{y}_i$ is the ith forecasted underlying asset price; y_i is the ith market the HSI.

As shown in Table 2.1, average errors of the Heston model are smaller than the CEV model, which means Heston, with an adaptive correlation coefficient scheme, works better than the CEV model in respect of one-day-ahead prediction of the underlying price. Furthermore, we also estimate the distribution performance of our model. The underlying price distribution is a measure of future price based on the term structure. In our test, we measure it over a horizon of 79 days of price distribution. The MAE of our model is nearly three times less than that of CEV model. We also compare the precision of trend prediction of our model with CEV model. As shown in Table 2.1, our model has 62.82 percent of the trend prediction precision over the 79-day period while the CEV model has only 56.41 percent.

Table 2.1 One-day ahead comparison

Model	*Distribution errors*	*Trend prediction (%)*	*One-day-ahead errors*
CEV	2810.8	56.41	1393.35
Heston	375.90	62.82	211.92

2.5 Conclusions

Prediction of the underlying asset price has always been a hot and interesting topic in academic research on financial markets. Different from the traditional time series method, we estimated distribution of the underlying price in a different way, using a model-free implied volatility term structure. We first introduced the stochastic model in Section 2.2 and found that stochastic volatility is most suitable for prediction of the underlying price. Before simulating distribution of the underlying price, we calculated the model-free implied volatility term structure. Finally, we simulated distribution of the underlying price based on the term structure. Our results are better than the CEV model in terms of one-day-ahead prediction performance and the 79-day distribution of the underlying asset price.

3 An adaptive correlation Heston model for stock prediction

The traditional Heston model assumes that the correlation between the underlying asset price process and volatility process is constant. This chapter investigates this correlation and proposes an adaptive correlation coefficient scheme to estimate the Heston parameters. The performance of adaptive correlation in the Heston model is compared with a traditional Heston model in terms of prediction precision.

3.1 Introduction

3.1.1 Background

Heston (1993) proposed a stochastic model for option pricing – the Heston model – which considers the process of the underlying asset price as a Geometrical Brownian movement with volatility as a stochastic process. The process of volatility takes the long-run mean of volatility into consideration, which ensures that volatility varies within a reasonable range. This overcomes the disadvantages of the Black–Scholes (BS) model, which is constrained to several assumptions. Furthermore, Heston assumed a constant correlation between the underlying price process and a stochastic volatility process. This makes sure the underlying price evolves reasonably.

However, after observation of market data on the Hang Seng Index (HSI), we have found that the correlation coefficient is not necessarily a constant. It varies from time to time. Coefficients of volatility process, including rate of reverting to mean level, the long-run mean volatility level, and the volatility of volatility, vary time-dependently, which ensures the process of volatility evolves within a corrective process. Therefore, we apply the Heston model with a dynamic correlation coefficient to establish a deterministic relationship between the underlying price and volatility.

3.1.2 Motivations

We find that the constant assumption does not hold in the HSI market. Figure 3.1 shows comparison of the Hang Seng Volatility Index (VHSI) and the HSI from June 2008 to July 2011. The solid line represents the time series data of the HSI.

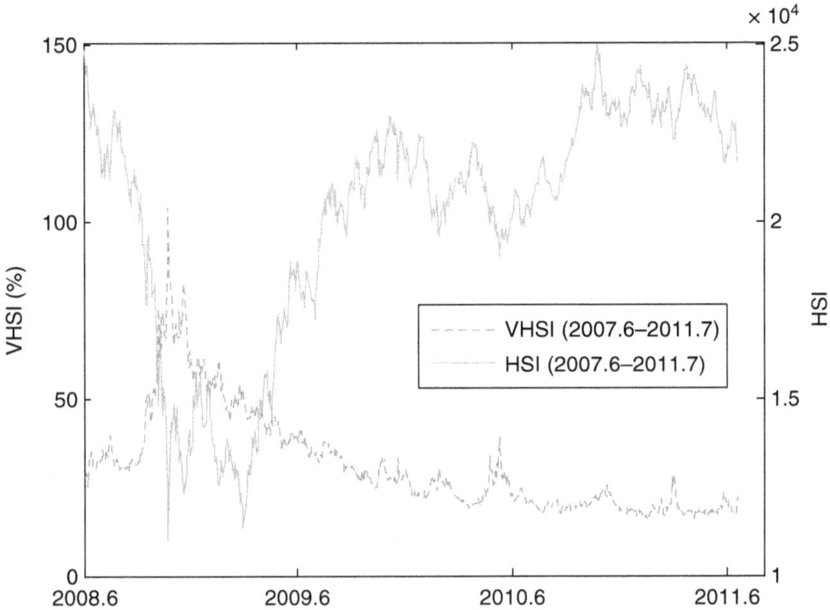

Figure 3.1 Time series of the VHSI and the HSI.

The dashed line represents the time series of the VHSI. The two are obviously highly correlated. When the HSI went down in the period June 2008 to November 2008, the trend of the VHSI was obviously upward. When the HSI climbed from March 2009 to November 2009, the VHSI also declined gradually. When the price fluctuated from January 2010 to July 2011, the VHSI also experienced high fluctuations.

To numerically analyze the correlation between the VHSI and the HSI, we use Pearson's correlation coefficient which defines the correlation as the covariance of two variables divided by the product of their standard deviation.

$$\rho_{X,Y} = \frac{cov(X,Y)}{\sigma_X \sigma_Y} = \frac{E\left[(X-\mu_X)(Y-\mu_Y)\right]}{\sigma_X \sigma_Y} \tag{3.1}$$

Here, in our analysis, X represents the series of the VHSI, Y represents the series of the HSI. We divide the time series data into four sections and calculate their respective correlation coefficients. Table 3.1 shows that different sections have different time periods and the correlation coefficients are also different from each other. Furthermore, the number of observations affects the correlation coefficients.

Correlation coefficients of sections 1 and 3 are relatively high. Their numbers of observations are also low. Section 4 also has a correlation of −0.5937 but its number of observations is high. As is known, observations over a long period of

Table 3.1 Correlation coefficients between the VHSI and HSI

Section no.	*Time period*	*Correlation coefficient*	*Number of observations*
1	June 2008~November 2008	−0.9629	120
2	December 2008~March 2009	0.0974	80
3	April 2009~November 2009	−0.8858	160
4	December 2009~July 2011	−0.5937	409

time may be unable to capture the trend of time series. Nevertheless, section 2 has observations over a short period but its correlation is also low. That is because the trend of this section is fluctuating and unstable. The above analysis suggests that the correlation coefficient may be affected by two factors:

1 The number of observations affects the correlation coefficient. If the observation period is too large, the correlation coefficient is affected severely.
2 The trend of the underlying asset price should be monotonous. If the process of underlying asset price fluctuates during the observation period, the coefficient also changes dramatically.

Therefore, a suitable length of time observing and a stable time series trend are critical for obtaining a high correlation coefficient. In the next section, we propose an adaptive correlation coefficient scheme to capture the correlation between the underlying price process and the volatility process.

3.2 Adaptive correlation coefficient model

3.2.1 Adaptive correlation Heston model

Compared with the BS model, Heston (1993) assumes a European option with strike price K and time to maturity T can be priced by using the following equation. This is a closed-form solution for the Heston model (Moodley, 2005).

$$C(S_t, V_t, t, T) = S_t P_1 - K e^{-r(T-t)} P_2 \tag{3.2}$$

where

$$P_j(x, V_t, T, K) = \frac{1}{2} + \frac{1}{\pi} \int_0^\infty \mathrm{Re}\left(\frac{e^{-i\varphi \ln(K)} f_j(x, V_t, T, \varphi)}{i\varphi} \right) d\varphi$$

$$x = \ln(S_t)$$

$$f_j(x, V_t, T, \varphi) = \exp\{C(T-t, \varphi) + D(T-t, \varphi)V_t + i\varphi x\}$$

$$C(T-t, \varphi) = r\varphi i T + \frac{a}{\sigma^2}\left[\left(b_j - \rho\sigma\varphi i + d\right)\tau - 2\ln\left(\frac{1-ge^{dr}}{1-g}\right)\right]$$

$$D(T-t,\varphi)=\frac{b_j-\rho\sigma\varphi i+d}{\sigma^2}\left(\frac{1-e^{dr}}{1-ge^{dr}}\right)$$

$$g=\frac{b_j-\rho\sigma\varphi i+d}{b_j-\rho\sigma\varphi i-d}$$

$$d=\sqrt{(\rho\sigma\varphi i-b_j)^2-\sigma^2\left(2u_j\varphi i-\varphi^2\right)}$$

For $j=1,2$, we have

$$u_1=\frac{1}{2},\quad u_2=-\frac{1}{2},\quad a=\kappa\theta,\quad b_1=\kappa+\lambda-\rho\sigma,\quad b_2=\kappa+\lambda$$

Thus, Heston's method seems to be suitable for pricing of European options. However, as mentioned above, we observe that the correlation coefficient between the underlying asset price and volatility is not constant. It varies with time and the shape of the stochastic process. Therefore, we propose to use the principle of least squares method to estimate the correlation coefficient.

From the market option data, we already know the option prices. Then, we can use (3.2) to estimate the option price and compare the results with real market data. We rewrite the function of (3.2) as follows:

$$C(S_t,V_t,t,T)=F\left(S_t,V_t,t,T,K;\kappa,\theta,\sigma,\rho\right) \tag{3.3}$$

where parameters of S_t, V_t, t, T, K are already known, or can be calculated from real options market data. Here, we define a vector $\alpha=[S_t, V_t, t, T, K]$. The parameters of $\kappa, \theta, \sigma, \rho$ need to be estimated. We define a parameter vector $\beta=[\kappa,\theta,\sigma,\rho]$. The difference between the estimated option price and the real option price is $r_i=y_i-F(\alpha_i,\beta)$, where y_i is the ith real option price. The squared summation of the difference is Φ:

$$\Phi=\sum_{i=1}^{n}r_i^2=\sum_{i=1}^{n}\left(y_i-F\left(\alpha_i,\beta\right)\right)^2 \tag{3.4}$$

where n is the total number of options data. According to the spirit of the least squares method, if the first differential of (3.4) is equal to 0, Φ will arrive at an optimal value. That is,

$$\frac{\partial\Phi}{\partial\beta_j}=2\sum_{i=1}^{n}r_i\frac{\partial r_i}{\partial\beta_j}=-2\sum_{i=1}^{n}r_i\frac{F(\alpha_i,\beta)}{\partial\beta_j}=0 \tag{3.5}$$

where $j=1,2,3,4$ corresponds to the parameter index of β. By solving Equation (3.5), we finally obtain an optimal parameter group, including the optimal correlation coefficient.

3.2.2 Distribution of the underlying asset price

In Section 3.2.1, we proposed an adaptive correlation coefficient scheme in the Heston model. By using historical options data, we are able to estimate the optimal parameters in the Heston model. Given these parameters, stochastic processes of the underlying asset price and volatility are specified from the Heston model. However, since the process of volatility is calculated from historical options data, which does not reflect the current or future market view of investors, the process of the underlying price calculated by the volatility process also lacks future market information. Therefore, we use the volatility term structure as the long-run mean level of the Heston model to solve this problem because the volatility term structure incorporates a market view of the future options market. Then, the underlying price process is calculated from this volatility process.

In the basic Heston model, the underlying asset price is determined by a stochastic process with a constant drift rate and stochastic volatility. Stochastic volatility is another stochastic process but has a correlation with the first process. Therefore, the underlying process is very similar to the geometric Brownian process (GBP). In GBP, the underlying asset price process is a stochastic process with a constant drift rate and constant volatility. Stochastic differential equation (SDE) of GBP is as follows:

$$dS_t = \mu S_t dt + \sigma S_t dW_t \tag{3.6}$$

where μ is the percentage drift rate. Basically, the drift rate is equal to the risk-free interest rate minus the stock dividend. σ is percent volatility. They are both assumed to be constant in the assumption of geometric Brownian movement. W_t is a standard Wiener process.

In our model, we have already incorporated the implied volatility term structure. The term structure of interest rate is also available from HIBOR. For a given time t and initial stock price S_0, an analytic solution can be derived from SDE of (3.6) by applying Ito's interpretation (Ito, 1951):

$$S_{t+1} = S_t \exp\left(\left(\mu_t - \frac{V_t}{2}\right)t + \sqrt{V_t}W_t^S\right) \tag{3.7}$$

where S_t is the stock price at time t. The right hand side of (3.7) represents the calculation of the future stock price based on the initial value. For a given time t, the implied volatility is obtained from the volatility term structure described above. μ_t is the drift rate, a function of time t. According to Heston (1993), the drift rate of the stochastic process is equal to the interest rate minus the stock market dividend, namely, $\mu_t = r_t - D_t$. W_t^S is a Wiener process generated by normal distribution with mean of 0 and variance of 1. However, since W_t^S has an optimal correlation with W_t^V, they are calculated as follows:

$$W_t^V = \sqrt{dt}\varepsilon$$

$$W_t^S = \rho_t W_t^V + \sqrt{1-\rho_t^2}\sqrt{dt}\varepsilon \tag{3.8}$$

where ρ_t is the dynamic correlation coefficient of the Heston model. Similarly, a stochastic process of implied volatility based on term structure is generated as follows:

$$V_{t+1} = V_t \exp\left[\left(\kappa(\theta - V_t) - \frac{\sigma^2}{2}\right)dt/V_t + \frac{\sigma W_t^V}{\sqrt{V_t}}\right] \tag{3.9}$$

where κ is the mean reversion speed; θ is the long run mean level of implied volatility, which can be obtain from the term structure; σ is volatility of volatility.

3.3 Empirical tests

3.3.1 CEV model

The constant elasticity of variance (CEV) option price model was proposed by Cox (1975). It includes the BS model as a member. Cox assumed that the underlying price process is a stochastic process driven by a stochastic differential equation:

$$dS_t = \mu S_t dt + \sigma S_t^{\gamma} dW_t \tag{3.10}$$

where μ, σ, and γ are constant parameters, satisfying conditions of $\sigma \geq 0$ and $\gamma \geq 0$. At any given time t, standard deviation of returns is defined as follows:

$$V_t = \sigma S_t^{(\gamma-2)/2} \tag{3.11}$$

Therefore, the "CEV exponent" (Emanuel and MacBeth, 1982) γ determines the relationship between volatility and the underlying price. When γ equals to 2, volatility equals the constant variable σ. This is the standard BS model and the option price in CEV model is the same as in the BS model. When γ is less than 2, we can see the leverage effect from (3.11), which means the underlying price increases while volatility decreases. By contrast, when γ is greater than 2, this is the so-called inverse leverage effect, where volatility rises with increase of the underlying price.

Based on the stochastic differential Equation (3.10), we can draw the distribution of the underlying asset price from stochastic volatility as follows, in accordance with geometric Brownian motion (GBM).

$$S_{t+1} = S_t \exp\left[\left(r_t - \frac{1}{2}\left(\frac{V_t}{S_t^{1-\gamma}}\right)^2\right)t + \frac{V_t\sqrt{t}W_t^S{}^{1-\gamma}}{S_t}\right] \tag{3.12}$$

where r_t is the risk-free interest rate.

In this section, we combine (3.11) and (3.12) and use the Monte Carlo simulation to calculate distribution of the underlying price. Given the initial underlying price S_0, we can calculate the initial volatility by applying (3.11). Iteratively, the next day price is computed from the volatility of the previous day, using (3.12).

3.3.1.1 Empirical analysis

As mentioned in Section 3.3.1, the CEV model contains the constant parameters μ, σ, and γ in which μ is equal to the interest rate since we assume there are no dividends during the period. σ is volatility of volatility. Therefore, we calculate σ from the time series and consider σ as the standard deviation of the term structure. Then, there is a unique sigma each day. According to Ncube (2009), the value of γ is important because γ determines the relationship between volatility and the underlying asset price. Similarly, we set γ equal to 0.5.

Before we simulate the volatility process of the CEV model, it is important to discretize it. In this simulation, the forecasting step of CEV model uses day as unit, measured by year. There are 21 trading days in a month, which means there are 21 volatilities in one month. By using Monte Carlo simulation, we generate the volatility process. Furthermore, when generating random numbers for simulation, we set the random seed of normal distribution at 11 and calculate the random term of the underlying asset price process from these random numbers. At each evaluation day, once we use the underlying price to generate the volatility, according to (3.12), we can use the volatility to estimate the underlying price of the next day. The first underlying price is from market data.

The Heston model is a stochastic volatility model. Parameters of the Heston model affect the volatility process greatly. Hence, in order to obtain an optimal group of parameters, we train the Heston model by using historical options data from 2 January 2007 to 30 November 2009. Data for the last month of the market option are left for testing. Section 3.2.1 discussed the four parameters of $\beta = [\kappa, \theta, \sigma, \rho]$ to be estimated. In our empirical running results, we obtain the optimal as follows, using the algorithm described in Section 3.2.1:

$$\hat{\kappa} = 1.746, \quad \hat{\theta} = 0.306, \quad \hat{\sigma} = 0.499, \quad \hat{\rho} = -0.899$$

Implied volatility is a measure of future average volatility, which reflects the degree of anxiety on part of investors, about future prices of options and stocks. The volatility term structure, therefore, contains significant information about market view. The Heston simulation based on the term structure, therefore, becomes significant. To make use of the historical options market data, we simulate the Heston volatility process by using the term structure as the long-run mean of volatility. The above optimal parameters are also used in simulation of the volatility process.

As described in Section 3.2.2, the underlying price process is also a stochastic process and has a correlation with the volatility process. The optimal correlation coefficient is -0.899, which is dynamically estimated by the least squares method.

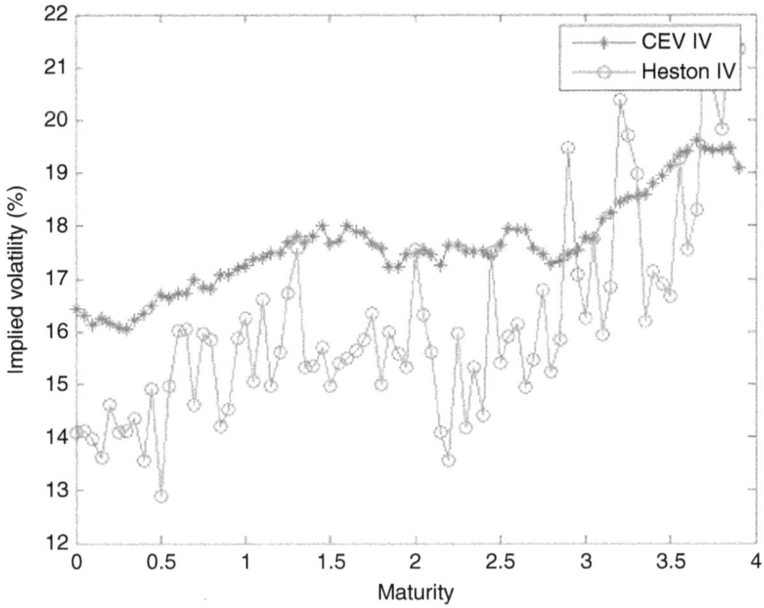

Figure 3.2 CEV implied volatility vs Heston implied volatility.

Table 3.2 One-day ahead comparison

Model	*79 days errors*	*One-day ahead errors*
CEV model	2810.8	1393.35
Heston model	375.90	211.92

By using this parameter, we simulate the Heston model and the CEV model. In Figure 3.2, the star line is the CEV implied volatility. The circled line is the process of Heston volatility.

As shown in Table 3.2, the average error of the Heston model is smaller than the CEV model, which means the Heston model with an adaptive correlation coefficient scheme works better than the CEV model for prediction of one-day-ahead underlying price. Furthermore, we also estimate the distribution performance of our model. The underlying price distribution is a measure of future price based on the term structure, which we measure over a horizon of 79 days, in the test. The MAE of our model is nearly three times less than that of the CEV model.

3.4 Conclusions

The Heston model is a stochastic volatility model that has advantages when used to simulate the time series of the underlying price. In this chapter, we first introduced the characteristics of the Heston model and then proposed an adaptive correlation coefficient scheme since the constant correlation of the Heston model is unsuitable for the HSI and the the VHSI. In the empirical test, we compared our adaptive correlation scheme with the CEV model on both a 79-day horizon prediction and a one-day-ahead prediction. The results of the adaptive correlation Heston model are better than the CEV model in terms of one-day-ahead prediction performance and the 79-day distribution of the underlying price.

4 The algorithm to control risk using options

Options as a financial derivate perform well in arbitrage. Because of the leverage, it is also a powerful tool for risk management. Options can change the return distribution and control risk effectively. However, their complexity always keeps investors away from using options to control risk. This chapter uses basic theories of options and the method of simulation to clarify the significant role options can play in risk management. Different characteristics and effects of different options are analyzed by applying different options to investment.

4.1 Introduction

The option as a financial derivative can be used not only in arbitrage but also in risk management. It is a derivative that specifies a contract between two parties for a future transaction at a reference price. The buyer of the option gains the right, but not the obligation, to engage in that transaction, while the seller incurs the corresponding obligation to fulfill the transaction.

Because of some special characteristics such as monetary leverage, it can perform well in risk management. Options can play an important role in risk management. From the first option traded in CBOE in April 1973, option has developed significantly over the past decades. Since Black and Scholes (1973) proposed an option pricing model, called Black–Scholes (BS) model, the option trading has been popular.

After decades of development, the option is now playing a significant role in financial markets because of some particular characteristics. Though it has many characteristics, such as leverage, which are good for risk management, the option is now used more widely for arbitrage because of its complexity and investors' disregard of risk management. It is well known that options can increase the flexibility of returns available from investment strategies and can truncate the downside risk efficiently. So the option as a powerful risk management tool has been widely accepted.

However, few works have focused on this field. Most investors and scholars put their eyes on the profit, which results in risk management being ignored. The characteristics of options were first explored by Merton *et al.* (1978, 1982). After that Bookstaber and Clarke (1983, 1984) developed their theory using Monte Carlo simulation and the Capital Asset Pricing Model (CAPM) to analyze the impact of option on return distribution. They used CAPM to state the influence of the option and in their paper they also proved the function of the option in risk management. Both call and put can change return distribution. Put is useful in truncating the downside risk. The limitation of their papers is that they just illustrated the characteristics of options. They did not prove why the option changed the return distribution and did not suggest the way to choose the right option to control risk. Ahn *et al.* (1997) solved this problem. Their target was to reduce VaR by using put option based on cost C. If the cost is limited, they try to find a balance point between the hedge rate and the exercise price of put to minimize VaR. This chapter aims to expand the method of risk management and combine both the target of reducing the potential risk and raising profit by using both put and call options. Because options are powerful in changing the return distribution and making the return flexible, they can provide more choices and extend the efficient frontier for different investors to meet their different risk appetites.

This chapter is composed of four main parts. The first part is the introduction which illustrates the background and previous research in this field. The second part is the theoretical background and the methodology. It can be divided into two parts. The former is the theoretical basis to use the method to analyze risk management with use of option, while the latter is the model to solve the problem by using option to control the risk and get more profit. The third part discusses the advantages and disadvantages of these two methods. The last part is the conclusion. In this part, the results are analyzed to support risk management.

4.2 Theoretical background and model

4.2.1 Theoretical background

Because of its special characteristics, the option is widely accepted as a good tool for risk management, especially the put option, which can truncate downside risk efficiently. The BS model is popular in trading options. Geometric Brownian motion (GBM), also known as exponential Brownian motion, is a continuous-time stochastic process in which the logarithm of the randomly varying quantity follows a Brownian motion (Ross, 2007), also called a Wiener process. The BS model is useful for calculating the reference value of the option. The model in this chapter is based on the assumption that the change of the underlying asset's value, S_t, always follows a stochastic process called the GBM. The equation can be written as the following stochastic differential equation:

$$dS_t = \mu S_t dt + \sigma S_t dW_t \tag{4.1}$$

where μ and σ are the drift and the diffusion of the asset value, and W_t is a standard Brownian motion. In fact, most assets can be simulated in this process, whether it is a single asset or a portfolio of assets, such as the Hang Seng Index. The GBM process can better simulate the change in asset value. For any time period t, parameters of μ and σ can be calculated and for the initial value S_t, the analytic solution of Equation (4.1) can be derived based on Ito's Lemma, which is

$$S_{t'} = S_t \exp\left(\left(\mu - \frac{\sigma^2}{2}\right)(t' - t) + \sigma W_{t'}\right) \tag{4.2}$$

where $S_{t'}$ is the value of the asset at t' after a time step Δt. The conditional distribution of asset $S_{t'}$ is alognormal distribution:

$$\ln S_{t'} \sim N\left[\ln S_t + \left(\mu - \frac{\sigma^2}{2}\right)\Delta t, \sigma^2 \Delta t\right] \tag{4.3}$$

The probability density function of $S_{t'}$ is

$$f_{s_t'}(s;\mu,\sigma,\Delta t) = \frac{1}{\sqrt{2\pi}}\frac{1}{s\sigma\sqrt{\Delta t}}\exp\left(-\frac{\left(\ln s - \ln S_t - \left(\mu - \frac{\sigma^2}{2}\right)\Delta t\right)^2}{2\sigma^2\Delta t}\right) \tag{4.4}$$

Equation (4.2) can be used to simulate the change of the asset value. It is a reference for the investor to make a decision and can be tested for different investment strategies. Equation (4.4) is the distribution of asset value in time period t' without any risk control. In the next part, this chapter uses different risk management strategies using options, which change the return distribution efficiently. The model proposed in this chapter is helpful to analyze different risk management strategies quantitatively to help investors find proper strategies to control risk. In the following part, both put and call options are taken into consideration to build the model to analyze the different impacts these two kinds of options can have in risk management.

4.2.2 A risk management model

The change characteristics of asset and return distribution have been stated above. Here, we build a risk management model using options. First, we use the put option to control risk and, in the second part, we use the call option. Finally, we compare the two methods to demonstrate their advantages and disadvantages.

4.2.2.1 Risk management model using put option

In the model where the put option is bought to control risk, an assumption is made that the capital being consumed needs to be less than a fixed cost C. Usually the optimal ratio h, corresponding to fixed cost C is less than 1. The first reason is that the main objective is to control risk. If ratio h is bigger than one, costs in excess of one can be used for a higher exercise price option which can affect a larger range of the distribution and performs better. The second reason is that if there is no higher exercise price option, the part that is higher than one can be divided and this can be viewed as the arbitrage using option and be analyzed singly.

Assume the strategy is buying an option with exercise price X, at price P_p. The hedging rate can be expressed as

$$h = f(p_P) \tag{4.5}$$

In reality, the price and the exercise can be obtained from the market, but it is necessary to use the model to find the best balance point as a reference. It is well known that the BS model performs well for calculating the price of the option. So the equation using this model can be expressed as

$$C = hf\big(BS(S_t, X, r, \Delta t, \sigma, y)\big) \tag{4.6}$$

In this equation, r is the risk free rate and y is annualized, continuously compounded yield of the underlying asset over the life of the option. Equation (4.6) has been solved by Ahn *et al.* (1997). In reality, the continuous solution is not necessary. Because the number of put options that can be chosen is never too large, combinations of h and X are enumerated if ratio h is viewed as discrete. This is not different from choosing the best strategy by comparing all of these choices. In this chapter, the relationship between h and X is necessary for further research. The return distribution can be divided into two conditions, when using the option with exercise price X. The underlying asset price in time t', $A_{t'}$, can be defined into the format of a piecewise function:

$$\begin{cases} A_{t'} = S_{t'} & \text{if } S_{t'} \geq X \\ A_{t'} = hX + (1-h)S_{t'} & \text{if } S_{t'} < X \end{cases} \tag{4.7}$$

Combining Equations (4.4) and (4.7), the probability density function of the hedged future value of asset $A_{t'}$ can be defined as

$$\begin{cases} f(A_{t'} \mid s_{t'} \geq X; \mu, \sigma, \Delta t) \\ = \frac{1}{\sqrt{2\pi}} \frac{1}{A_{t'}\sigma\sqrt{\Delta t}} \times \exp\left(- \frac{\left(\ln A_{t'} - \ln S_t - \left(\mu - \frac{\sigma^2}{2}\right)\Delta t\right)^2}{2\sigma^2 \Delta t} \right) \\ f(A_{t'} \mid s_{t'} < X; \mu, \sigma, \Delta t) \\ = \frac{1}{\sqrt{2\pi}} \frac{1-h}{(A_{t'} - hX)\sigma\sqrt{\Delta t}} \times \exp\left(- \frac{\left(\ln(A_{t'} - hX) - \ln(1-h) - \ln S_t - \left(\mu - \frac{\sigma^2}{2}\right)\Delta t\right)^2}{2\sigma^2 \Delta t} \right) \end{cases} \tag{4.8}$$

All parameters in the equation above can be calculated at time t, except for h and X, which are decision variables. The relationship between these two parameters can be expressed in Equation (4.6), at a given cost C.

4.2.2.2 *Risk management model using call option*

The option, as a good tool of risk management, has always been ignored in reality. Some works have explored the use of the put option in risk management. It is well known that both call and put options can change the return distribution effectively. Bookstaber and Clarke (1983, 1984) also proved that the call option has the function of controlling risk and raising profit. The Wing Fung Financial Group, for example, earns most of its profit from selling options. It is effective at selling call options to get the premium and reduce risk to a certain degree. Accordingly, the distribution of the hedged future value of underlying asset can be built to analyze the function of selling call options in risk management.

The problem can still be divided into two conditions. The option either finishes out- or in-the-money. The difference between using call and put option to control risk is that when using the call option, the hedged ratio h does not relate to cost C because the premium on selling the call option can hedge the risk to some extent. This means that once the strategies of investment have failed, the premium on selling the call option can hedge some of the risk caused by the investment. But the hedged ratio h affects both conditions, at-the-money and out-of-the-money. In this model, the hedged value of the asset can be defined as

$$\begin{cases} A_{t'} = hX + (1-h)S_{t'} + P_c & \text{if } S_{t'} \geq X \\ A_{t'} = S_{t'} + P & \text{if } S_{t'} < X \end{cases} \tag{4.9}$$

Parameter P_c is the premium earned from selling call option and it can be calculated as

$$P_c = hf'(BS(S_t, X, r, \Delta t, \sigma, y)) \tag{4.10}$$

In this model the assumption of h is made the same as the model of put option. Combining Equations (4.4) and (4.10), the distribution of the hedged future value of the asset can be calculated as

$$\begin{cases} f(A_{t'} \mid s_{t'} \geq X; \mu, \sigma, \Delta t) \\ = \frac{1}{\sqrt{2\pi}} \frac{1}{(A_{t'} - P_C)\sigma\sqrt{\Delta t}} \times \exp\left(-\frac{\left(\ln A_{t'} - \ln S_t - \left(\mu - \frac{\sigma^2}{2}\right)\Delta t\right)^2}{2\sigma^2 \Delta t} \right) \\ f(A_{t'} \mid s_{t'} \geq X; \mu, \sigma, \Delta t) \\ = \frac{1}{\sqrt{2\pi}} \frac{1-h}{(A_{t'} - hX)\sigma\sqrt{\Delta t}} \times \exp\left(-\frac{\left(\ln(A_{t'} - hX) - \ln(1-h) - \ln S_t - \left(\mu - \frac{\sigma^2}{2}\right)\Delta t\right)^2}{2\sigma^2 \Delta t} \right) \end{cases} \tag{4.11}$$

Combining Equation (4.11) into Equation (4.10), the probability density function of the asset value can be calculated and it can be viewed as the impact of using the call option in risk management. But this model is more complicated than that of the put option. Comparing Equations (4.6) and (4.10), it is clear that the parameter of cost C is given as a fixed number, while P_c in the equation is an independent variable which depends on parameters h and X. In reality, the parameter is in the interval from zero to one, and the exercise price X of call option is also limited. So it is not difficult to find the suitable range of h and X.

Up to now, the impact of both the call and put options can be given mathematically and in detail. From Equations (4.7) and (4.9), we can directly draw the conclusion that options can help improve the value of the underlying asset. That means it has the function of risk management. Furthermore, from Equations (4.8) and (4.11), it is obvious that options can change the return distribution and improve the return in bad cases. Of course, both methods have advantages and disadvantages. This is summarized in the next part.

4.3 Discussion

In this part, the advantages and disadvantages of both methods are discussed. By summarizing these, the characteristics of the two methods can be viewed directly and it is helpful to promote the use of options in risk management.

4.3.1 Advantages of method one

First, using the put option in risk management has been accepted widely as it can truncate the downside risk effectively. Especially in extreme cases, it can keep the risk within a range. Second, for any given cost C, it is easy to find the optimal strategy to control risk and simulate the impact the strategy can make. Third, the capability of this method is bigger than the method of using the call option. This cost C can always keep the risk within an ideal range.

4.3.2 Disadvantages of method one

This method is just like insurance. The application of this method always leads to a cost. It performs well only in extreme cases. What's more, the impact the method can make is decided by cost C. Since the capital that can be used in this method is limited, the impact the method can make is also limited.

4.3.3 Advantages of method two

While using the call option in risk management, in most cases the investor can not only keep the risk within a certain range but also earn excess profits. Moreover, this method is not limited by cost. In reality, this method performs well in most cases.

4.3.4 Disadvantages of method two

It is obvious that the boundary of risk in this method is P_c and if the value of the asset rises to the upper bound, this method reduces the profit. The domain in which the method can perform well is limited, i.e. in extreme cases this method has limited effectiveness. What's more, because of the complexity of the model itself, it is more difficult to find the optimal strategy than when using method one.

In summary, both methods can change the return distribution well and can extend the efficient frontier to meet the different risk appetites. Both of them can make VaR and CVaR less when applied into the investment.

4.4 Conclusions

This chapter has provided a formal analysis of risk management using different kinds of option and constructed two models to analyze the different functions of the different methods. By analyzing the role of the option in risk management, the conclusion that can be drawn is that the option is a good tool for the investor to use in risk management. It is well known that options can increase flexibility of returns and this can affect the return distribution directly. What's more, options have the characteristic of leverage. All of the above make the option a good tool in risk management.

Equation (4.7) in model one and Equation (4.9) in model two showed that options always help improve the value of the underlying asset in bad cases. That means both put and call options have the function of risk management. Furthermore, Equations (4.8) and (4.11) in models one and two described the roles of put and call options in risk management briefly. In the third part both the advantages and disadvantages of these two methods were discussed, when using them to control risk. Most importantly, this is the first paper to state the function of both put and call options in risk management, to build a model to illustrate them and compare the two methods. Of course there still is a lot of work that needs to be done in the future. It may be possible to use real data to prove these two methods are useful in risk management and use real data to prove that these two methods can perform well in risk control in some aspects.

5 Option strategies

Evaluation criteria and optimization

For a specified underlying asset, a large number of options can be chosen, especially for the combined strategies. Compared with stock, designing strategies for option trading for arbitrage is more complex. In reality, most investors design strategies empirically. This chapter uses the Hang Seng Index (HSI) as the underlying asset and uses some standard criteria such as VaR, CVaR, and so on as references to build a model for design of optimal strategies for investment. A real case is also used to prove that good results can be obtained, based on a good prediction of the trend of the HSI.

5.1 Introduction

The option plays a significant role in financial markets and it is widely used in both arbitrage and risk management. As one kind of financial derivative, it is an instrument that specifies a contract between two parties for a future sale or purchase of an asset at an agreed price. The buyer of an option gets the right, but not the obligation, to engage in that transaction, while the seller is bound to fulfill the corresponding obligation.

Because of some special features such as leverage, it can perform well in investment for both arbitrage and risk management. Since it was first traded, unified and standardized in CBOE in April 1973, the option as an instrument has developed significantly over the past few decades. When Black and Scholes (1973) created the model of pricing the option in their paper "The Pricing of Options and Corporate Liabilities," trade in options has boomed. The model is called Black–Scholes (BS) model and is still widely used. Most of research works are done by using this model as the foundation. In this chapter, this model is used to calculate the theoretical price of the option. In terms of flexibility of using the option in investment and its functions, Bookstaber and Clarke (1983, 1984) have proved that the option is powerful in changing the distribution of returns. These two papers also point out that the appropriate option strategies can always meet requirements of investors. Apart from the function of changing the return distribution, the option itself is a wonderful tool for investment and it is gaining increasing acceptance among investors. Though using option for arbitrage has been very popular and its share in financial markets has been growing, almost all financial organisations design their strategies empirically.

In reality, investors trust their experience more than quantitative analysis and so usually draw a trend line based on their experiences, market view and a little data analysis. Then they find options which stay away from the line, which can create space for arbitrage. This method always works if the trend line is accurate but it is limited in some aspects. First, the strategies are not based on quantitative analysis and, therefore, usually they are not the optimal strategies. The fund utilization rate is low and it can ensure benefit maximization only under certain conditions. Second, because these strategies are designed empirically, it is impossible to get hold of the risk level. The option itself is complex and results in the need for constant changes in strategies. Many books have been written to illustrate the characteristics of option strategies (Bookstaber and Clarke, 1983). The option is helpful for investors to control the different strategies but facing the option in the market, designing and choosing the right strategy is still a big problem. In order to address this issue, this chapter builds a model and uses quantitative analysis to solve the problems of designing option strategies empirically.

This chapter uses the the HSI's options as an example, so the foundation of building the model is a good prediction of the HSI. The predicting data in this chapter is the result of a distortion of Monte Carlo simulation which has been proved accurate in most cases. In fact, all financial companies have their own ways of predicting the market and they trust the prediction to a certain degree. The main objective of this chapter is to build the model to solve the problem of designing option strategies empirically. So it is assumed that the market trend predicted in this chapter is accurate.

The model in this chapter is built to solve the problems of designing option strategies empirically. Some standard measures are used to build the model, such as VaR, CVaR, expected return, return rate, and so on. There are, usually, scores of options to choose from at any given time. What's more, the complex strategies which combine different options can result in a number of possible strategies running into the thousands. The model in this chapter can rank the different strategies and provide different efficient frontiers by the measures mentioned above. Different evaluation criteria are calculated as references for investors with different risk appetites. It is easy for investors to estimate potential risks and benefits to optimize their investment strategies.

This chapter is composed of four main parts. The first is the introduction which outlines the background, describes previous research works in this field and illustrates the basic concepts and the significance of building the proposed model. The second part is the theoretical background and the model. In this part, the theory and the process of building the model are described. The third part is the result of the model. In this part, the result is discussed and the model is demonstrated to be useful in reality, by using real cases. The last part is the conclusion which summarizes the significance of this chapter and the meaning of the model proposed in this chapter.

5.2 Theoretical background and model

The model proposed in this chapter is based on the HSI, implying that the option strategies yielding profit depends on the trend of the HSI. The option is a European style option which has an expiration date T and can only be executed at the expiration date but can be traded on the market as a kind of merchandise. It has been mentioned that investors who use option strategies for arbitrage usually try to find the option which strays away from its normal value and earn the difference in value by buying and selling the option. There are dozens of option strategies which can be used for arbitrage and it is impossible to list all in one paper. However, according to the position of an option, it can be divided into four kinds of basic styles and composite types. In this chapter, four kinds of basic style are discussed and one kind of composite type is chosen as an example to build the model.

5.2.1 The model of basic style

Here we build the model of a strategy short call. A short call means selling a contract wherein the buyer of the contract has the option to buy the underlying asset at the agreed price at the expiration date. The payoff of this kind of strategy can be expressed in piecewise functions. It can be defined as

$$payoff = \begin{cases} n \times p_c^t & S_T \leq K_c \\ n \times p_c^t - n \times (S_T \leq K_c) & S_T > K_c \end{cases} \tag{5.1}$$

In this equation, *payoff* is the profit derived by selling a call option. P_c^t is the price of each call option at time t. K_c is the strike price of this call option. S_T is the price of the underlying asset at the time of expiration. The first part is that the contract becomes out-of-the-money while the other part is at-the-money. For the sake of simplicity, parameter n is assumed to be "1" in the rest of this chapter.

In fact, investors who use options for arbitrage usually use short-swing trading, which means the strategy is generally stopped before expiration. In this condition, the payoff can be defined as

$$payoff = P_c^t - P_c^{t'} \tag{5.2}$$

where parameter $P_c^{t'}$ means the value of the call at time t' and $t < t' < T$. It is impossible to predict values of $P_c^{t'}$. It has been mentioned above that the BS model is popular for calculating the price of options. So $P_c^{t'}$ can be obtained from the function

$$P_c^{t'} = blsprice(S_{t'}, K_c, r, T - t', v, y) \tag{5.3}$$

In Equation (5.3), r is annualized, continuously compounded risk-free interest rate of return and v is annualized asset price volatility. y is annualized, continuously compounded yield of the underlying asset and in this chapter it is assumed to be zero. So in Equation (5.3), once $S_{t'}$ and v are estimated, value of $p_c^{t'}$ can be calculated.

In this chapter, $S_{t'}$ and v are predicted by using a kind of Monte Carlo simulation. The result of the Monte Carlo simulation is a distribution of $S_{t'}$. The expected payoff of this strategy is expressed as

$$E[payoff] = \sum_{i=1}^{n} (p_c^t - p_c^{it'}) P(S_{t'}^i) \tag{5.4}$$

$P(S_{t'}^i)$ means the probability of value of the underlying asset $S_{t'}^i$ at time t' being $P(S_{t'}^i)$. The expected payoff is one of the evaluation criteria. In Equation (5.4), parameter $P_c^{it'}$ can be replaced by Equation (5.3). The expected return is only dependent on distribution of the underlying asset. In the following part, VaR, CVaR, and the return rate are calculated to meet varying risk appetites of different investors.

The definition of VaR is a threshold value that defines the maximum mark-to-market loss on the portfolio over the given time horizon. In this problem, it can be expressed as

$$VaR_\alpha(payoff) = -inf\{l \in R\colon F_{payoff}(l) \geq \alpha\} = p_c^t - p_c^{jt'} \quad j = n\alpha \tag{5.5}$$

where j is the jth $P_c^{jt'}$ after ranking the $P_c^{jt'}$ in accordance with order of return from bad to good. Using the same method, CVaR can be expressed as

$$CVaR_\alpha(payoff) = \frac{1}{\alpha}\left[\sum_{i}^{j} (p_c^t - p_c^{it'}) P(S_{t'}^i)\right] \quad j = n\alpha \tag{5.6}$$

All parameters in Equation (5.6) have the same assumptions and meanings as in Equation (5.5). The last evaluation criterion which needs to be calculated in this model is the return ratio. In the models in this chapter, the methods to calculate this parameter are different for different strategies.

For strategies of selling the option, there is no definition of input-output ratio, but there is a ratio of potential income and risk, so the ratio can be viewed as the quotient of expected return divided by the potential loss

$$R = \frac{E[payoff]}{\left| \frac{1}{\sum_i^k P(S_{t'}^i)} \left[\sum_i^k (P_c^t - P_c^{it'}) p(s_{t'}^i)\right] \right|} \tag{5.7}$$

where k is the number which, if $i \leq k$, the return corresponding to $S_{t'}^i$ is negative, otherwise the return is positive.

As to the strategies of buying option, it can be defined as

$$R = \frac{E[payoff]}{C} \tag{5.8}$$

where C is the cost of buying the option.

5.2.2 *The model of the composite style*

The model of composite style can be viewed as a combination of different basic styles. In this chapter, the composite style of a bull spread is used as an example. In option trading, a bull spread is a bullish, vertical spread options strategy that is designed to profit from a moderate rise in the price of the underlying security. Because of put–call parity, a bull spread can be constructed using either put options or call options. If constructed by using calls, it is a bull call spread, otherwise it is a bull put spread. The bull call spread is constructed by buying a call option with a low exercise price, k_{c1}, and selling another call option with a higher exercise price, k_{c2}. They usually have the same expiration date. There are dozens of call options that can be chosen to construct this kind of strategies. The number of this kind of strategy can be very large and it is impossible for investors to analyze and find the optimal strategy for arbitrage. It is the simplest strategy in composite style. As to strategies such as butterfly and condor, constructed with four or more basic styles, the number is sizeable. They are more difficult to analyze. So, evaluation criteria are necessary for investors to find the optimal strategy for arbitrage.

In the following part the bull call spread is used as an example of composite style. The model of the bull call spread strategy is derived from the model of short call to calculate the evaluation criteria of this strategy. As to the other composite, it can be derived from the model of the short call, the same as this strategy. The notation system and assumptions are the same as in the model above. Moreover, the lower exercise price call option is marked with the subscript "1," while the other is marked "2." The payoff can be expressed as

$$payoff = \begin{cases} P_{c2}^{t} \times n_{c2} - P_{c1}^{t} \times n_{c1} & S_t \leq K_{c1} \\ (S_t - K_{c1}) \times n_{c1} + P_{c2}^{t} \times n_{c2} - P_{c1}^{t} \times n_{c1} & K_{c1} < S_t \leq K_{c2} \\ (K_{c2} - K_{c1}) \times n_{c2} + P_{c2}^{t} \times n_{c2} - P_{c1}^{t} \times n_{c1} & K_{c2} < S_t \end{cases} \tag{5.9}$$

This is the same as the model above. In reality it is usually short-swing trading for arbitrage and for the sake of simplicity, assume $n_{c1} = n_{c2} = 1$. Then Equation (5.2) for this model is

$$payoff = \left(p_{c1}^{t'} - P_{c1}^{t}\right) + \left(P_{c2}^{t} - P_{c2}^{t'}\right) \tag{5.10}$$

In Equation (5.10) parameters of $P_{c1}^{t'}$ and $P_{c2}^{t'}$ can also be calculated by using the BS model, described in Equation (5.3). Moreover, the expected payoff of this strategy is as follows:

$$E[payoff] = \sum_{i=1}^{n} \{[(P_{c1}^{it'} - P_{c1}^{t}) + (P_{c2}^{t} - P_{c}^{it'})]P(s_{t'}^{i})\} \tag{5.11}$$

It has been mentioned above that distribution of the underlying asset $S_{t'}$ and the parameters in the BS model can be obtained by using a Monte Carlo simulation. Then the expected return can be calculated by substituting Equation (5.3) into the equation above. Of course, the evaluation criteria of VaR, CVaR, and the return ratio also need to be calculated. The model to calculate these criteria can be derived from the model above.

The mathematical equation of VaR for this strategy is

$$\begin{aligned} VaR_{\alpha}(payoff) &= -inf\{l \in R\colon F_{payoff}(l) \geq \alpha\} \\ &= (P_{c1}^{jt'} - P_{c1}^{t}) + (P_{c2}^{t} - p_{c2}^{jt'}) \quad j = n\alpha \end{aligned} \tag{5.12}$$

The parameters in this equation have the same meanings as in Equation (5.5).

The mathematical equation of CVaR for this strategy is:

$$CVaR_{\alpha}(payoff) = \frac{1}{\alpha}\left[\sum_{i=1}^{i}\left((P_{c1}^{jt'} - P_{c1}^{t}) + (P_{c2}^{t} - P_{c2}^{jt'})\right)P(S_{t'}^{i})\right] \quad j = n\alpha \tag{5.13}$$

The definition and assumptions of VaR and CVaR are the same as the model in the basic style part but the method of calculating the return ratio is different from the former. The return ratio of this strategy can be calculated by using Equation (5.9). This strategy is constructed by buying a lower exercise price call option and selling a higher exercise price call option; the two options have the same expiration date and the same underlying asset. In these two kinds of option, the lower exercise always has the higher price. So constructing this kind of strategy always leads to a cost. So the return ratio depends upon the condition that the input-output ratio can be calculated by using Equation (5.9) described when building the model of return ratio in the basic style part. This can be written as

$$R = \frac{E[payoff]}{P_{c1}^{t} - P_{c2}^{t}} \tag{5.14}$$

The expected payoff is calculated in Equation (5.11) and the denominator is the cost incurred for constructing this strategy.

In this part, two models have been built to support investment for arbitrage by trading options. The first is the model for the basic style while the other is for the composite style, constructed by a different option. For other strategies, the models can be built in the same way. There are many options trading in the market at any given time, and the number of different combinations of these strategies is huge. It is impossible to find a suitable strategy for arbitrage. In the above model, four evaluation criteria are proposed for automatic optimization of the strategy and to meet different risk appetites by ranking the strategies based on different criteria.

5.3 Results

In this part, a real case is used to prove the validity of the model. We made the Monte Carlo simulation on 28 September 2011 to predict the trend of the HSI. In fact, distribution of the HSI can be obtained by this simulation. The means are described in Figure 5.1, which presents the trend of the HSI as predicted by Monte Carlo simulation.

The conclusion that can be drawn from the figure is that the HSI will rise in the next 120 days but it will drop in the next few days. So it can be derived that for short-term investment in options for arbitrage, selling a call or buying a put will yield a profit. In the former part, four evaluation criteria are pointed out and the model is built to calculate these four criteria to help investors identify the optimal strategy. Here, we use one of the four criteria, VaR, as an example to rank the basic option strategies as a reference for investors.

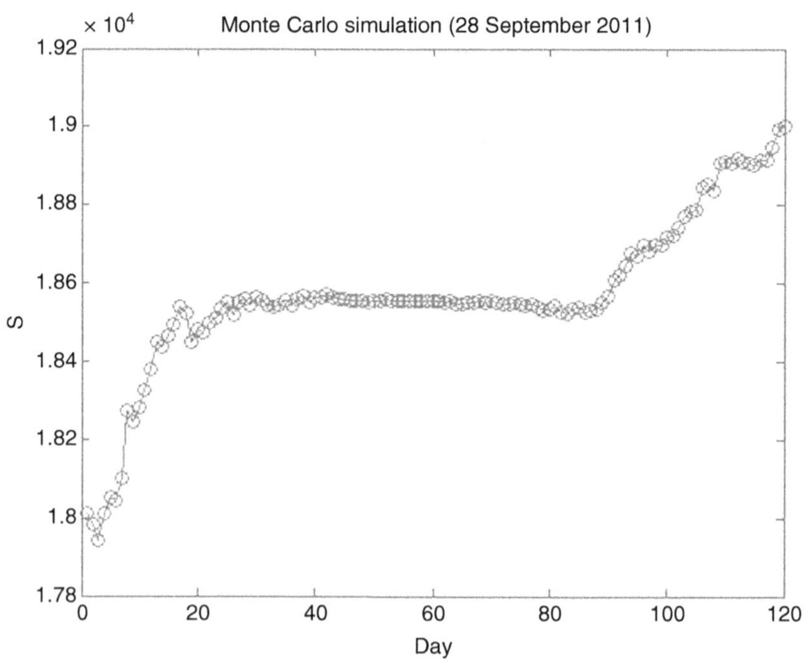

Figure 5.1 Result of Monte Carlo simulation.

Table 5.1 Ranking of basic style by VaR

	Expiration date	*Code name*	*VaR*	*Sharpe ratio*
Short call	November 2011	C18800	813.237	0.811
	November 2011	C19000	807.176	0.883
	November 2011	C20000	802.545	0.968
Long call	December 2011	C18400	−10.000	0.475
	December 2011	C20200	−14.000	0.478
	December 2011	C19800	−19.999	0.474
Short put	December 2011	P14600	−49.000	0.950
	November 2011	P17400	−68.000	0.876
	December 2011	P17800	−100.000	0.837
Long put	December 2011	P16400	899.975	0.934
	November 2011	P15800	897.999	0.997
	December 2011	P8800	896.626	1.000

Table 5.2 The result of using option strategies for arbitrage

Contract	*28 September 2011*	*30 September 2011*	*Payoff*	*Return rate*
Short HSI November 2011 C18000	639	470	165	25.9%
Long HSI November 2011 P16400	586	687	101	17.2%

Table 5.1 lists the results of ranking of the four basic styles by the order of VaR. Some basic information is also listed in the table. Based on this the optimal strategy for arbitrage is selling the call option C18800 or buying the put option P16400. By observing the real date of option as on 28 September 2011 and 29 September 2011, the result of using these two option strategies for arbitrage is as listed in Table 5.2. This table proves that these two strategies are wonderful for arbitrage and that the model is useful to support use of options for arbitrage. This can work well if the trend of the underlying asset can be predicted accurately.

The results illustrated above are just for the four basic style option strategies of arbitrage and only results ranked by VaR are listed. In fact, the model can work for all option strategies such as bull spread, butterfly, condor, and so on and all the evaluation criteria can be calculated easily. They are useful criteria for investors to design effective option strategies for arbitrage and can help the investor to find the optimal option strategy.

5.4 Conclusions

This chapter has proposed automatic design of option strategies, using evaluation criteria, to support investors in finding the optimal strategy in the area of using options for arbitrage. The option has been widely viewed as a powerful tool in both risk management and arbitrage but the complexity of its usage always keeps investors away. This is a big stumbling block in the development of the option as a financial instrument. Though considerable research has been conducted to introduce the method of using option strategy, few works have used standard criteria to evaluate the effects of different strategies and there is no work which can support the investor in design of the optimal strategy automatically. Traditional investors usually design their strategies empirically, which brings in a lot of problems. This chapter has constructed models (illustrated in the second part) to solve this problem. The model was divided into two parts: basic and composite. The validity of the models is demonstrated by applying them to real data and the results were shown in the third part of this chapter.

Though this chapter has made a great contribution to both evaluation and optimization of option strategies used for arbitrage, the information the model can provide is not enough. In future work, information of the parameters of Greeks in options can be provided, which will make the model integrated and more effective.

6 A novel mean reversion-based local volatility model

Local volatility is deterministic volatility, which is a function of the underlying asset price and time. If the local volatility and time are given, the underlying asset price can be calculated from this function. This chapter proposes a novel local volatility model with a mean-reversion process and overcomes the weakness of traditional local volatility. After the local volatility has been precisely modeled, a surface fitting scheme is used to recover the local volatility surface.

6.1 Introduction

The mean-reversion phenomenon of stock prices was first proposed by Keynes (1936) that "all sorts of considerations enter into market valuation which are in no way relevant to the prospective yield" (p. 152). When stock prices diverge from the long-run mean level, they eventually return. The larger the deviation is, the higher is the probability they will return. Cecchetti *et al.* (1990) found that the asset price usually vibrated within a 60 percent confidence interval of its long-run mean level and the asset price finally returns to its mean level.

Hence, the mean-reversion process is common in the stock market. Bessembinder *et al.* (1995) studied the term structure of commodity futures prices and concluded that the mean reversion process exists in an asset price time series. Engle and Patton (2001) found that the mean-reversion phenomenon also existed in volatility of asset price when they sought a model to predict volatility. That is, high volatility of the underlying asset price eventually evolves into its long run mean level. In this chapter, we focus on the evolution of local volatility of the underlying asset price and propose a novel local volatility model with a mean-reversion process.

Dupire (1994) presented a deterministic equation to calculate the local volatility from option price based on the assumption that all call options with different strikes and maturities are priced in a consistent manner. Sepp (2002) used market implied volatility to extend Dupire's local volatility formula. However, from our empirical analysis, we find that both of these models are unstable. The local volatility calculated from these models may reach 800 percent or above in some cases. This is irrational. To address these weaknesses, we propose a novel robust local volatility model with a mean-reversion process. Based upon the traditional local volatility model, we design a mean reversion term and plug into a traditional formula. With this term, when the computed local volatility is too high or too low, our model can revert it and make local volatility return to its long-run mean level.

6.2 Motivations

Local volatility is the deterministic function of the underlying asset price and time. This means local volatility has the ability to forecast the future stock price trend. Most of the current literature has focused on improving the computational precision of local volatility. Coleman *et al.* (1999) used spline to present the local volatility function. They obtained this function by solving a nonlinear optimization problem to closely fit these option prices. Crépey (2003) found that local volatility obtained from real option prices was usually unstable. He proposed the Tikhonov regularization method to control local volatility and minimized the distance between calibration price and market price to get optimal Tikhonov regularization parameters.

However, some scholars have applied mean reversion to improve the local volatility model. Black (1990) proposed that a volatility model with mean reversion can help interpret why volatility and the risk premium decline when wealth rises. Fouque *et al.* (2000) found that the stochastic volatility reverted slowly to its mean level but fast when the maturity was large. Feng *et al.* (2010) analyzed Heston's stochastic volatility model and found that the maturity was large when compared to the rate of mean-reversion. In this chapter, we propose that the local volatility model also owns the property of mean reversion. The more local volatility deviates from its mean level, the greater is the rate at which the local volatility reverts.

After precisely modeling local volatility, we use the Monte Carlo simulation to estimate the future stock trend. We use the normalized distribution with mean of the risk-free interest rate and variance of the local volatility. Finally, the path-dependent trend of the stock price is simulated from local volatility.

6.3 Mean reversion-based local volatility model

6.3.1 Local volatility model

Local volatility is the deterministic function of the underlying asset price and time. Dupire (1994) proposed the local volatility model formula as follows:

$$\sigma_{loc}^2(K,T) = 2\frac{\frac{\partial C_{market}}{\partial T} + (r(T) - d(T))\,K\frac{\partial C_{market}}{\partial K} + d(T)\,C_{market}}{K^2\frac{\partial^2 C_{market}}{\partial K^2}} \tag{6.1}$$

Sepp (2002) used market implied volatility to express Dupire's local volatility formula as follows:

$$\sigma_{loc}^2(K,T) = 2\frac{\frac{\sigma_{imp}}{T-t} + 2\frac{\partial\sigma_{imp}}{\partial T} + 2(r(T)-d(T))K\frac{\partial\sigma_{imp}}{\partial K}}{K^2\left(\frac{\partial^2\sigma_{imp}}{\partial K^2} - d_1\sqrt{T-t}\left(\frac{\partial\sigma_{imp}}{\partial K}\right)^2 + \frac{1}{\sigma_{imp}}\left(\frac{1}{K\sqrt{T-t}} + d_1\frac{\partial\sigma_{imp}}{\partial K}\right)^2\right)} \tag{6.2}$$

where

$$d_1 = \frac{\ln(S/K) + \left(r(T) - d(T) + \frac{1}{2}\sigma_{imp}^2\right)(T-t)}{\sigma_{imp}\sqrt{T-t}}$$

However, in practice, we find that both of these equations are not stable, especially when using the long term expiry of options from the Hang Seng Index (HSI). The local volatility fluctuates greatly and suffers a lot from errors caused by implied volatility calculated from long term options. As is shown in Figure 6.1, local volatility has reached 800 percent when using a long term maturity option

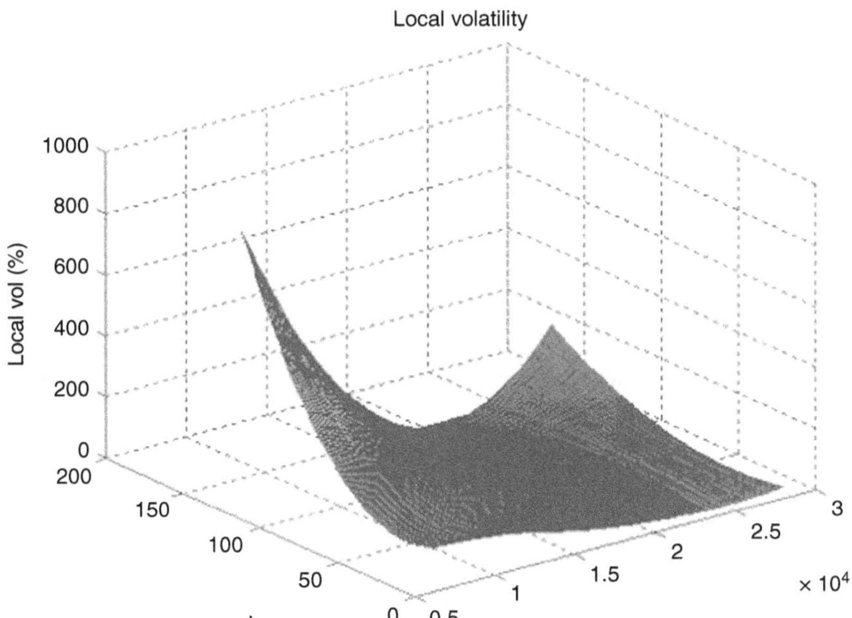

Figure 6.1 Local volatility surface.

and a large underlying asset price. Furthermore, there also exist many negative values of local volatility calculated from these two formulas.

Therefore, to fix this problem, we propose to add a mean-reversion term to Sepp's Equation when deriving local volatility from implied volatility. This mean-reversion term helps correct errors caused by computation. To make local volatility more robust, we consider the computation of local volatility with the existence of market shocks or jumps which ensure the local volatility model is more suitable to the realized market.

6.3.2 Mean-reversion process

As local volatility is a function of time and the underlying asset price, we fix the underlying asset price[1] and analyze the mean-reversion process of local volatility against time. Implied volatility is a function of maturity and strike price. However, the series of maturities of different options is discrete. In order to analyze the relationship between the underlying asset price and implied volatility, Sepp (2002) proposed a local volatility calculated from implied volatility based on Dupire's works. In his model, the local volatility is a function of continuous time. Hence, to improve this model, we propose a mean-reversion term and apply this term to local volatility model.

Assume that X_t is the long-run mean level of local volatility, θ is the reversion rate. The farther local volatility departs from its mean level, the greater the reversion rate will be. Based on this assumption, we formulate our novel local volatility with mean reversion as follows:

$$Y_t' = X_t + (Y_t - X_t)e^{-\theta|Y_t - X_t|} \tag{6.3}$$

where $X_t = \frac{1}{t}\sum_{i=1}^{t}\sigma_{loc}(S,i)$ and $\theta \geq 1$. θ can be determined from real market data. Y_t is the local volatility calculated by Sepp's formula. Y_t' is the volatility computed by our novel local volatility model. We view the distance between local volatility and its mean level as the departure degree. If this distance increases dramatically, the right hand side of (6.3) also decreases deeply. Hence, we assert that if the observed horizon is long enough, Y_t' will finally converge to its long-run mean level.

HYPOTHESIS 1 *If a local volatility is given with a mean-reversion process as follows,*

$$Y_t' = X_t + (Y_t - X_t)\,e^{-\theta|Y_t - X_t|}$$

Then, Y_t' will finally converge to its long-run mean level.

Proof:

$$\begin{aligned} E\left[Y_t'\right] &= E\left[X_t\right] + E[(Y_t - X_t)e^{-\theta|Y_t - X_t|}] \\ &= E\left[X_t\right] + E[Z_t e^{-\theta|Z_t|}] \quad (\text{where } Z_t = Y_t - X_t) \end{aligned}$$

$$= E[X_t] + \int_{-\infty}^{+\infty} Z_t^2 e^{-\theta|Z_t|} dZ_t$$

$$= E[X_t] + \int_{0}^{+\infty} Z_t^2 e^{-\theta Z_t} dZ_t + \int_{-\infty}^{0} Z_t^2 e^{\theta Z_t} dZ_t \qquad (\otimes)$$

In $\otimes$, we calculate two definite integrals as follows:

$$\begin{aligned}
&\int_{0}^{+\infty} Z_t^2 e^{-\theta Z_t} dZ_t \\
&= e^{-\theta Z_t} \int_{0}^{+\infty} Z_t^2 dZ_t + Z_t^2 \int_{0}^{+\infty} e^{-\theta Z_t} dZ_t \\
&= \frac{1}{3} Z_t^3 e^{-\theta Z_t} \Big|_0^{+\infty} - \frac{1}{\theta} Z_t^2 e^{-\theta Z_t} \Big|_0^{+\infty} \\
&= \lim_{Z_t \to +\infty} \frac{1}{3} Z_t^3 e^{-\theta Z_t} - 0 - \left(\lim_{Z_t \to +\infty} \frac{1}{\theta} Z_t^2 e^{-\theta Z_t} - 0 \right) = 0
\end{aligned}$$

$$\begin{aligned}
\int_{-\infty}^{0} Z_t^2 e^{\theta Z_t} dZ_t &= e^{\theta Z_t} \int_{-\infty}^{0} Z_t^2 dZ_t + Z_t^2 \int_{-\infty}^{0} e^{\theta Z_t} dZ_t \\
&= \frac{1}{3} Z_t^3 e^{\theta Z_t} \Big|_{-\infty}^{0} + \frac{1}{\theta} Z_t^2 e^{\theta Z_t} \Big|_{-\infty}^{0} \\
&= 0 - \lim_{Z_t \to -\infty} \frac{1}{3} Z_t^3 e^{\theta Z_t} + 0 - \lim_{Z_t \to -\infty} \frac{1}{\theta} Z_t^2 e^{\theta Z_t} = 0
\end{aligned}$$

Then, $\otimes$ can be modified as follows:

$$E\left[Y_t'\right] = E[X_t]$$

This means that for a long horizon of observations, the expected new local volatility will equal to that of the long-run mean level. Hence, the new local volatility will finally revert to its long-run mean level. □

Therefore, combining Equations (6.2) and (6.3), we propose our novel mean-reversion local volatility model as follows:

$$\begin{aligned}
\sigma_{loc}'(S,t)|_{S=S_0} = \frac{1}{t}\sum_{i=1}^{t} \sigma_{loc}(S,i) + \left(\sigma_{loc}(S,t) - \frac{1}{t}\sum_{i=1}^{t} \sigma_{loc}(S,i) \right) \\
\exp\left(-\theta \left| \sigma_{loc}(S,t) - \frac{1}{t}\sum_{i=1}^{t} \sigma_{loc}(S,i) \right| \right) \Bigg|_{S=S_0}
\end{aligned} \qquad (6.4)$$

where S_0 is a given underlying asset price.

After the local volatility is precisely modeled, we use Monte Carlo simulation to estimate future underlying asset price trend. We apply the normal distribution through the risk-free interest rate and variance of the local volatility. Finally, the path-dependent trend of the underlying asset price is simulated from local volatility.

6.4 Local volatility surface

Typically, Dupire (1994) presented a deterministic equation to calculate the local volatility from option price based on the assumption that all call options with different strikes and maturities should be priced in a consistent manner.

Nevertheless, this deterministic function also suffers two weak points. First, the shortcoming is intrinsic to Dupire's equation. The indeterminacy of the equation may cause local volatility on the left to be extremely large or very small. Second, because local volatility is a function of both strike and time to maturity and it is possible that same strikes are not available for each time to maturity and the number of local volatility is finite, which usually is not enough for further calculations and applications. As a result, researchers are inclined to interpolate to obtain a series data of local volatility for further calculations.

To fix the first problem, we propose a novel local volatility model with mean-reversion process described in the previous section. In this section, we focus on the second problem by using the Least Squares Method. We define a surface function $\varphi(x)$ as follows (the left hand side of the function represents the fitted local volatility):

$$\varphi(S,t) = \sum_{i=0}^{M-1}\sum_{j=0}^{T-1} A_{ij} S^i t^j \tag{6.5}$$

where A is a $M \times T$ matrix, S is the underlying asset price, and t is time, measured in years. Our aim is to find an optimal parameters matrix A such that the difference between fitted local and real local volatility is minimal. The errors function is defined as follows:

$$E_A = \sum_{k=1}^{N} \omega(S_i, t_j) \left[\sum_{i=0}^{M-1}\sum_{j=0}^{T-1} A_{ij} S_i t_j - \sigma(S_i, t_j) \right]^2 \tag{6.6}$$

where $k = 1, \ldots, N$, N means the total number of local volatilities, $\sigma(S_i, t_j)$ is the real local volatility with underlying asset price S_i and time t_j, and $\omega(S_i, t_j)$ is the weighted matrix at different points. Obviously, if we minimize the summation of errors, we will obtain an optimal parameters matrix for the surface function. Since a parabolic function can reach an optimal value at a given variable range, we differentiate (6.6) and get a partial differential equation of summation error function to a given parameter.

$$\frac{\partial E_A}{\partial A_{ij}} = 0 \tag{6.7}$$

We allow the partial differential result to be zero. In this way, the optimal value of the parabolic function is derived. After moving the real local volatility to the right hand side, (6.7) is transformed into (6.8).

$$\begin{pmatrix} (\varphi_{00}, \varphi_{00})(\varphi_{00}, \varphi_{01}) & \cdots & (\varphi_{00}, \varphi_{M-1T-1}) \\ \vdots & \ddots & \vdots \\ (\varphi_{M-1T-1}, \varphi_{00})(\varphi_{MT}, \varphi_{12}) & \cdots & (\varphi_{M-1T-1}, \varphi_{M-1T-1}) \end{pmatrix} \begin{pmatrix} A_{00} \\ \vdots \\ A_{M-1T-1} \end{pmatrix} = \begin{pmatrix} (\varphi_{00}, \sigma) & c \\ \vdots & c \\ (\varphi_{M-1T-1}, \sigma) c \end{pmatrix} \tag{6.8}$$

where $\varphi_{00} = S^0 t^0$, $\varphi_{01} = S^0 t^1, \ldots, \varphi_{M-1T-1} = S^{M-1} t^{T-1}$, $(\varphi_{00}, \varphi_{00}) = \sum_{k=1}^{N} S_k^0 t_k^0 \cdot S_k^0 t_k^0$, $(\varphi_{M-1T-1}, \varphi_{M-1T-1}) = \sum_{k=1}^{N} S_k^{M-1} t_k^{T-1} \cdot S_k^{M-1} t_k^{T-1}$, $(\varphi_{M-1T-1}, \sigma) = \sum_{k=1}^{N} S_k^{M-1} t_k^{T-1} \cdot \sigma_k$. The optimal parameters matrix A can be obtained by solving (6.8).

6.5 Empirical tests

The option price is the price of a contract which specifies a price that an underlying asset will be sold at a future given time. It is the difference between the current underlying asset price and future price at a given time. This means that this option price contains some views of investors or market participants on whether the market will go up or down in the future. In this chapter, we adopt the daily closing option prices of HSI provided by Hong Kong Exchanges and Clearing Limited (HKECL). Since the daily closing option price contains market information about the next day, next week, or even next month, this price also contains the power of predicting the future trend of the underlying asset price.

However, the data provided by HKECL usually contain noisy data also, which are useless for empirical study. Some data entries contain bid, ask, and closing price of options. But there is no trading volume. These prices do not reflect market views and should be considered as noisy data. Furthermore, when the trading day is close to the end of the month, prices of near expiry term options become abnormal. The local volatilities calculated from these option prices are also abnormal. To overcome this problem, we introduce an expiry rolling process to compute local volatility. Options are rolled to the next expired month starting from the fifth trading day prior to their current expired month. Moreover, when using option market data to calculate implied volatility, there is a rolling process for options due to expire. The rolling process is that the time to maturity of the current expiry

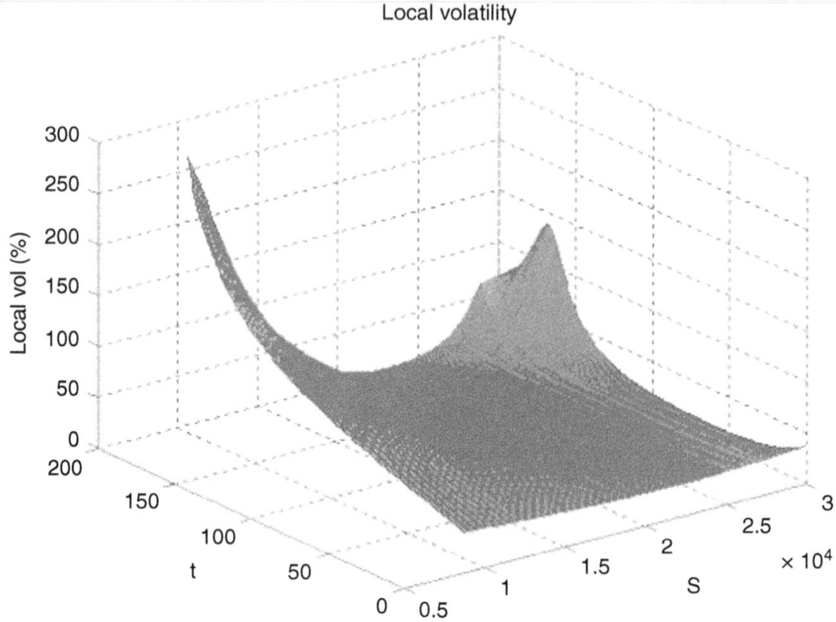

Figure 6.2 Volatility surface by traditional local volatility model.

month options with less than five trading days are calculated by using the expiry date of the next expiry month contract options as the expired date of these options.

As mentioned above, the Monte Carlo method is adopted to simulate the underlying asset price with local volatility as the variable. The analytic solution of stochastic differential equation of geometric Brownian motion shown as follows is used to calculate future prices:

$$S_{t+1} = S_t \exp\left(\left(\mu_t - \frac{V_t}{2}\right)t + \sqrt{V_t}W_t^S\right)$$
$$W_t^S = \sqrt{dt}\varepsilon \tag{6.9}$$

where S_t is the underlying asset price at time t. For a given price S_t, V_t is the corresponding local volatility at time t. μ_t is the drift rate, a function of time t. In this chapter, we use the HIBOR as the drift rate. W_t^S is a Wiener process, which is generated by normal distribution with mean of 0 and variance of 1. ε is a random term following a standard normal distribution.

To compare the performance of the mean-reversion local volatility model with the traditional local volatility model, we use forecasting power as a criterion. We compare the prediction power from three aspects, one-day-ahead prediction (ODA), five-day-ahead prediction (FDA), and price position prediction (PPP)

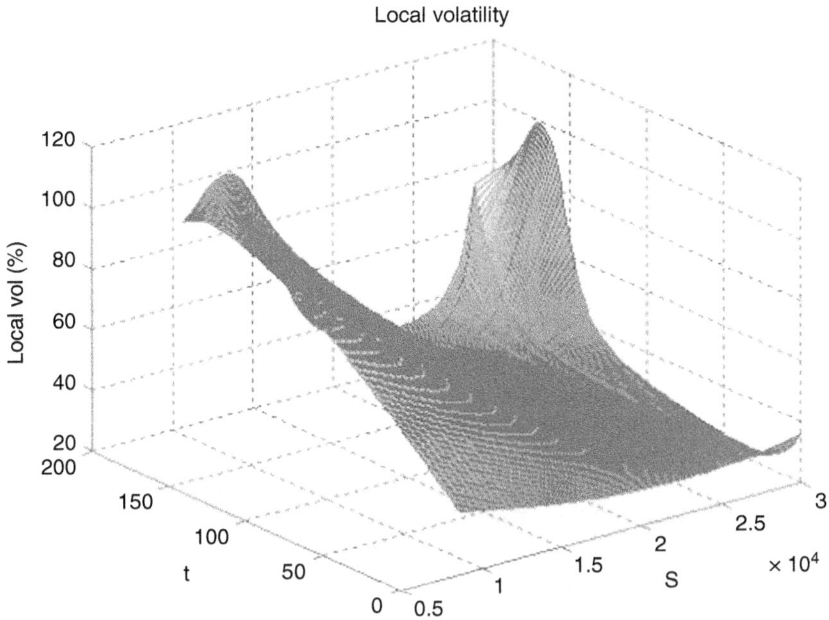

Figure 6.3 Volatility surface by mean-reversion local volatility model.

Table 6.1 Comparison of forecasting power

Model	*ODA*	*FDA*	*PPP*
Constant elasticity of variance (CEV) model	50.92%	49.75%	259.87
Traditional local volatility model	52.69%	51.46%	33.16
Mean-reversion local volatility model	57.79%	51.73%	65.01

precision. For position prediction precision, root mean square error is applied to measure average errors.

Figure 6.3 shows that our novel model can efficiently control local volatility within a rational range while the local volatility in Figure 6.2 varies greatly and departs far from its mean level. When comparing the forecasting power, we use the market option data from HKECL with a horizon of 17 months, from January 2011 to May 2012.

While comparing the position prediction precision, we use mean absolute error as the criteria. For one-day-ahead and five-day-ahead predictions (Table 6.1), our mean-reversion local volatility model has better performance. This means that as our model can control the local volatility variation within a rational range, there is little fluctuation after Monte Carlo simulation. The prediction of our model can be more stable than that of the traditional local volatility model. Furthermore, since we have constructed the three-dimensional surface for both mean-reversion and traditional local volatility models, the local volatilities are different at different days for simulation. However, CEV is a constant elasticity volatility model which assumes volatility of volatility is constant. This is unsuitable for real market conditions and hence, from the results of Table 6.1, we can find that the prediction power is poorer than the mean-reversion local volatility model.

6.6 Conclusions

From a review of the literature, it is found that few works have covered the application of the mean-reversion process to a local volatility surface. This chapter has proposed a novel mean-reversion local volatility model based on empirical study of the Hong Kong options market. Local volatility calculated from the traditional model is adjusted by a mean-reversion term. If the local volatility is far from its mean level, this term reverses it. The farther it departs from mean level, the greater is the rate it be reverted at. After that, least squares method is used as a surface fitting scheme to recover the local volatility surface. This surface is then used for a Monte Carlo simulation. For a given price, local volatility can be abstracted from the surface at different simulated times. Meanwhile, in the empirical tests section, the option price is processed by a rolling procedure. The expiries of options with a few trading days to expiry are rolled into the next expiry so that the local volatility computed by these options can be useful. Finally, our empirical tests results show that the prediction power of our mean-reversion local volatility model is better than that of traditional local volatility models and the CEV model.

7 Regression-based correlation modeling for the Heston model

In Chapter 3, the correlation of the Heston model is considered to be dynamic rather than constant assumed by the traditional Heston model. This chapter further explores this correlation and proposes a regression-based dynamic correlation Heston model. The correlation between volatility and the underlying asset price is estimated by three different regression models: simple regression model, polynomial regression model, and auto-regression model. Prediction performances of these models are compared in empirical tests.

7.1 Introduction

Heston is a stochastic model that assumes the underlying asset price and volatility of prices follow geometric Brownian motions. These two stochastic processes have a constant correlation. To further study the Heston model, Fonseca *et al.* (2008), Christoffersen *et al.* (2006), and Fruhwirth-Schnatter and Sogner (2008) proposed to model a variance process of the Heston model as a multifactor Wishart process and applied Fast Fourier Transform to price options. Benhamou *et al.* (2010) derived an accurate analytical formula for using the time-dependent Heston model to price vanilla options by extending the parameter of volatility of volatility. Furthermore, Sepp (2008) applied realized variance with the Heston model to price options and considered jumps of asset returns and variance. Though many other studies have focused on numerical simulation of Heston model, there is little literature on the correlation coefficient of the Heston model.

Saikat (1998), Perelló *et al.* (2004), and Kahl and Jackel (2006) studied the correlation of the Heston model and analyzed correlation of the Heston model as constant. Hobson (2004) and Asaia and McAleer (2009) considered the correlation coefficient as the dynamic parameter of the Heston model. Asaia and McAleer (2009) used the Markov Chain Monte Carlo procedure to estimate the dynamic correlation of the Heston model. However, all of them experienced great inconvenience and complications during real market operations.

Hence, to overcome these weaknesses, we propose a regression-based dynamic correlation Heston model. Our contributions are in two aspects. First, we consider the correlation of stochastic model as dynamic rather than constant. From the literature review, we find that most current studies are still focused on constant correlation of stochastic models. Second, we propose a multivariate regression model to estimate dynamic correlation of the Heston model. Although some recent papers have covered dynamic correlation, they are complicated and are not suitable for real time calculation, especially for high frequency trading. However, our model can be computed quickly and efficiently.

7.2 The Heston model

The Heston model is more complicated than the constant elasticity of variance (CEV). It takes the mean-reversion term into consideration and the assumption is that the two processes of the underlying asset price and volatility are stochastic processes with a constant correlation to each other. The original Heston model is defined as follows:

$$\begin{aligned} dS_t &= \mu(t)S_t dt + \sqrt{V_t}S_t dW_1 \\ dV_t &= \kappa(\theta - V_t)dt + \sigma\sqrt{V_t}dW_2 \end{aligned} \tag{7.1}$$

where θ is the long-run mean level of volatility, κ is the speed of instant volatility returning to long-run mean level, and σ is volatility of volatility. These three parameters satisfy the condition of $2\kappa_t\theta > \sigma^2$ and ensure the process of V_t is strictly positive. Furthermore, W_1 and W_2 are two standard Wiener processes and have a correlation of ρ.

As is mentioned in Section 3.1.2, the constant assumption is unsuitable for Hong Kong stock market. In Figure 3.1, when HSI moves upwards, the VHSI moves downwards. But this phenomenon is not constant. Especially after 2010, the two time series sometimes move towards a same direction. The time series of HSI has a correlation with VHSI. However, this correlation should be dynamic according to the results shown in Table 3.1. The factors may affect this correlation. They are the length of observation period and the trend of underlying asset price. Hence, different regression models are proposed in this chapter to estimate these two factors.

7.3 Regression-based correlation coefficient

The traditional Heston model and its extension usually consider the correlation as a constant variable. However, this assumption is unsuitable for real market conditions. In this chapter, we use the regression method to model the trend of the underlying asset price and volatility. Since during different time periods the underlying asset price and volatility have different series patterns, such as different parts of Figure 3.1, the observation lengths of time periods are optimized in the empirical tests section.

Luo and Zhang (2010) applied the regression method to examine the relationship of realized volatility, VIX, realized variance, historical volatility, and historical variance, and to obtain the information content of volatility term structure. However, they only forecast volatility rather than the underlying asset price.

Actually, we apply regression method to predict price by regressing the correlation of the underlying asset price and volatility. Through different regression models of correlation coefficient, the predicted prices are derived from volatility stochastic process. The performance of different regression models is compared in Section 7.4.

7.3.1 Simple regression

Different periods of observation have different series of patterns. The patterns are also affected by the observation period length. As shown in Figure 3.1, the series pattern of the HSI from March 2009 to June 2009 is like a linear pattern with a high correlation coefficient. So is the pattern of the VHSI in the same observed period. Hence, we use a simple regression model to estimate the correlation of the HSI and volatility as below:

$$S_t = \alpha_t + \beta_1 V_t + \varepsilon_t \tag{7.2}$$

where S_t is the underlying asset price, V_t is the stochastic volatility, and α_t specifies the expected position of the HSI. β_1 shows the unique effect of volatility on the HSI, the expected change of the HSI by a unit change of volatility.

7.3.2 Polynomial regression

Some series patterns can be modeled by simple regression. However, this is not always the case. If we measure the correlation of the HSI and volatility from March 2009 to March 2010, the linear regression is not suitable anymore. The series pattern is dropping down first and then climbing up. This series looks like a parabolic curve. Hence, we propose to use a polynomial regression model to measure the correlation for this pattern:

$$S_t = \alpha_t + \beta_1 V_t + \beta_2 V_t^2 + \varepsilon_t \tag{7.3}$$

where β_2 means the degree of effect of V_t^2 on the HSI. That is the expected change of the HSI for unit change of V_t^2. If β_1 is larger than β_2, this means V_t has a greater effect on the HSI. If β_1 is less than β_2, V_t^2 contains more information and has a greater impact on the HSI than V_t.

7.3.3 Autoregressive model

Although the polynomial regression model has a good performance for the parabola pattern, it is still not good enough for the vibrating pattern, such as the pattern from October 2010 to June 2011. The vibration mode is a more complicated pattern, which needs a complicated regression model. Since this pattern is vibrating, it has a center line and mean-reversion characteristics. So we propose to use an autoregressive model to evaluate this pattern, as follows:

$$S_t = \alpha_t + \beta_1 V_t + \beta_2 S_{t-1} + \varepsilon_t \tag{7.4}$$

where β_2 means the effect of S_{t-1} playing on asset price.

These three different regression models are applied to different series patterns. Different observation periods may also affect the series patterns. Hence, for a given observation length, we compare the error term of these models and select the suitable model with smallest regressive error. Then, we propose the following equation to capture the correlation coefficient:

$$\rho = \frac{2}{\pi} \mathrm{arctg}\beta \tag{7.5}$$

where ρ represents the correlation coefficient. β is the coefficient of regressive variant. For simple regressive model, β is equal to β_1. For polynomial regression, since the curvature reflects the instant change of correlation, β_2 is considered as β. For auto-regressive model, β_1 is considered as β.

In the basic Heston model, the underlying asset price is determined by a stochastic process with a constant drift rate and stochastic volatility, which is another stochastic process but has a correlation with the first process. Therefore, the underlying process is very similar to the geometric Brownian process (GBP). In GBP, the underlying asset price process is a stochastic process with a constant drift rate and constant volatility. Stochastic differential equation (SDE) of GBP is as follows:

$$dS_t = \mu S_t dt + \sigma S_t dW_t \tag{7.6}$$

where μ is the percentage drift rate. Basically, the drift rate is equal to the risk-free interest rate minus the stock dividend. σ is percent volatility. They are both assumed to be constant in the assumption of geometric Brownian movement. W_t is a standard Wiener process.

In our model, we have already incorporated the implied volatility term structure. The term structure of interest rate is also available from HIBOR. For a given time t and initial stock price S_0, an analytical solution can be derived from SDE of (7.6) by applying Ito's interpretation (Ito, 1951):

$$S_{t+1} = S_t \exp\left(\left(\mu_t - \frac{V_t}{2}\right)t + \sqrt{V_t} W_t^S\right) \tag{7.7}$$

where S_t is the stock price at time t. The right hand side of (7.7) represents the calculation of future stock price based on the initial value. For a given time t, the implied volatility is obtained from the volatility term structure described above. μ_t is the drift rate, a function of time t.

7.4 Empirical tests

In this section, the market option data from Hong Kong Exchanges and Clearing Limited (HKECL) are selected. The option data spanning from January 2011 to June 2012 are selected for analysis. However, before we apply this data for empirical tests, it needs to be cleaned from three aspects. First, options with price near the money are selected. Since the implied volatilities of options which are far out-of-the-money are irrationally large, these volatilities affect the regression models and cause noise in empirical tests. Second, the options with bid price small or equal to ask price are selected. Option data with bid price larger than the asking price are unreasonable. In the real market, the selling price should always be large or equal to the buying price. Hence, we consider this type of option data as noisy data and eliminate them. Finally, option prices with transaction volume are selected. Although some options have both a bid price and an ask price, there is no trading volume. These option prices are useless for tests.

The empirical tests contain in-sample data training and an out-of-sample test. There is a total 18 months of options data. The implied volatilities of these data are calculated from these data. The weights of implied volatility of each day during the testing period are computed according to a fix weighting scheme. We use a period of 12 months to train the Heston model with dynamic correlation. The volatility and underlying asset price are regressed according to the three different models described above. The regression training period is a key parameter. If it is too small, the polynomial efficient can be solved by regression. If it is too large, the data pattern will become complicated and affect regression results. Hence, we choose to search the optimal observation period, from three days to three months.

Since different regressive models are suitable for different data series patterns, they need different observation periods. Hence, three regressive models are trained. The correlation coefficient is calculated from the regression results according to Equation (7.5). According to Heston (1993), the drift rate of the stochastic process is equal to the interest rate minus the dividend, e.g. $\mu_t = r_t - D_t$. W_t^S is a Wiener process, generated by standard normal distribution. However, since W_t^S has an optimal correlation with W_t^V, they are calculated as follows:

$$\begin{aligned} W_t^V &= \sqrt{dt}\varepsilon \\ W_t^S &= \rho W_t^V + \sqrt{1-\rho^2}\sqrt{dt}\varepsilon \end{aligned} \tag{7.8}$$

where dt is the time interval of the term structure (measured in years); ε is the standard normal distribution variable; ρ is the correlation of these two processes. Similarly, the stochastic process of implied volatility based on term structure is generated as follows:

$$V_{t+1} = V_t \exp\left[\left(\kappa\left(\theta - V_t\right) - \frac{\sigma^2}{2}\right)dt / V_t + \frac{\sigma W_t^V}{\sqrt{V_t}}\right] \tag{7.9}$$

where κ is the mean reversion speed; θ is the long run mean level of implied volatility which can be obtained from the term structure; σ is volatility of volatility. These parameters can be obtained from historical options data.

For out-of-sample tests, we use data spanning January 2012 to June 2012, six months, to test the prediction performance of the three regression models.

One-day-ahead prediction is the forecast of the underlying asset price by the Heston model for one day. Five-day-ahead means predicting the underlying asset price for five days. One-month-ahead is to forecast for a period of one month. Furthermore, we also search for the optimal testing period for different regression models. As is shown in Table 7.1, the optimal regressive period is nine days. The effect of volatility playing on the underlying asset price is −2.16, which is −0.724 when modified by Equation (7.7).

From Table 7.1, we find that the correlation of simple regression is larger than the correlation of the other two models. This means that the simple regression model can better capture the correlation of the underlying asset price stochastic process and the volatility stochastic process than the other two regression models. For the polynomial regression model, the square of volatility has a higher correlation with the underlying asset price than volatility. The coefficient of the square of volatility also shows the instant changing speed of volatility. For auto-regression, it shows that the underlying asset price has autocorrelation. However, this autocorrelation affects the effect of volatility playing on underlying asset price.

Table 7.2 shows the comparative prediction performances of the regressive models. A simple regression model has a one-day-ahead prediction performance of 56.1 percent, which is better than the other two models. This is because simple regression has a small regression period and can capture the correlation precisely. Since the weighted implied volatility reflects the future views of market participants, this volatility owns some implied information content which can tell what the future market will be. When a simple regression model accurately captures this correlation, it then can predict more precisely than the other two models. By

Table 7.1 Coefficient comparison of regression models

	Coefficient				
Model	α	β_1	β_2	ρ	*Period*
Simple regression	19451.5	−2.16	–	−0.724	9
Polynomial regression	18568.3	−0.23	−1.97	−0.701	20
Auto-regression	12732.6	−1.66	0.32	−0.655	42

Table 7.2 Prediction performance comparison of regression models

	Performance		
Model	*One-day-ahead*	*Five-day-ahead*	*One-month-ahead*
Simple regression	56.1%	53.7%	51.3%
Polynomial regression	55.4%	52.3%	51.7%
Auto-regression	53.4%	50.9%	48.9%

comparing the other two prediction standards, we find that a simple regression model has a better performance.

7.5 Conclusions

Extant literature on the Heston model has mostly focused on a multivariate stochastic process. Although some studies have considered correlation of the Heston model as a stochastic process, this method is complicated and time-consuming; hence, unsuitable for real time calculations. However, we propose to use a regression model to estimate the correlation of the underlying asset price and volatility. The volatility is calculated from implied volatility with a fixed weighting scheme. Furthermore, three different volatility models are used to estimate the correlation. From our empirical tests, we find that the simple regression model outperforms the other two regression models.

8 Index option strategies

Comparison and self-risk management

VaR and CVaR are the criteria commonly used to evaluate potential risk to investors. For risk management, buying or selling underlying assets is useful for hedging potential risk. But as to the index option, this method does not work because of the difficulty of absolutely hedging against the movement of the index. Fortunately, it is possible for investors to hold the risk within a certain range by using the option itself. This is called self-risk management in this chapter.

8.1 Introduction

An option is a contract. This contract gives the buyer or seller a right to buy or sell the underlying asset at a fixed price and at a fixed time. It contains the ability to hedge risk and plays a role in risk management. Much work has been done to analyze the function of the option in changing the return distribution and controlling the risk. The put option especially can always truncate the downside risk of the underlying asset efficiently and the covered call is also useful to reduce the volatility of return. Though the option is used more for arbitrage than risk management, compared with stocks, funds, and bonds, investment in options usually faces a higher risk.

Regrettably, most work focused on the features of the option is relevant to risk management rather than the risk of the option itself. Management of option risk is usually more difficult than using the option to control risk. As to the equity option, by buying or selling a combination of the underlying asset and option, risk can be controlled to a certain degree, but in index options it is hard to control risk well because there is no product which can hedge the movement of the index. Though there are some products such as index futures which can hedge risk partially, it is hard to control it dynamically. Of course, there is a lot of research which has analyzed how to control option risks dynamically, such as the research about hedging the parameters of Greeks, but it works only in theory most of the time; in reality it is impossible to keep the state dynamically and it is very complex to construct this kind of portfolio.

This chapter provides new insights into option strategies and analyzes the potential risks of different strategies. Theoretically, the risk of the writer of an option is unlimited while that of the buyer is limited. This characteristic is used for truncating the downside risk and by using this characteristic, many strategies can be constructed to meet the demands of the investors when they want to invest in different market conditions such as bear, bull, straddle, strangle, butterfly, condor, and so on. Some of the combinations can limit risk, though a cost has to be incurred to do that. The advantage of this method is that risk management does not need other products and the risk can be held within a range. So by using this kind of strategy, it is called self-risk management.

What the investors usually care about is the expected return (ER) and a risk they can afford. So ER and some risk criteria are used in this chapter when the strategies are selected. VaR and CVaR are the criteria which are usually used in reality. By trading on the Hong Kong market, we know that for the Hang Seng Index (HSI) option, thousands of contracts are traded every day and almost all are at-the-money options. Only the at-the-money option has liquidity. Some statistical methods have been used to analyze the return of option strategies. Moreover, the analysis results pointed out that selling out the money put always has a higher return when using the option in arbitrage. But this is not enough. The HSI moves rapidly and a single position always leads to a huge loss. Some investors make a profit by constructing a portfolio to earn the time-decay value. This method of constructing a portfolio can have an important influence on returns. There are dozens of options strategies and there are hundreds of options which can be used to construct strategies.

Most previous works have depended upon statistical research to analyze the probability of getting profit by using these strategies. This chapter chooses the ER, VaR, and CVaR as the criteria to choose option strategies under the assumption that the movement of the HSI follows the geometric Brownian motion and then one needs to analyze the performance of different strategies for getting profit and managing the risk.

Results presented here can be the references for constructing portfolios in different conditions. Calculating the VaR and CVaR of these strategies can help investors know the potential risk and control it better. Compared with the method of setting the stop points, normally used in the trading of index options, these strategies can help construct portfolios which can hold the risk within a range. This means investors can build positions where the risk is pre-calculated. As to these strategies, the different positions can hedge the risk of each other so it can be called self-risk management.

8.2 Review

Since it was first traded unified and standardized in CBOE in April 1973, the option has developed significantly over the past few decades in both risk management and arbitrage. Since Black and Scholes (1973) created the model to price the option and presented it in their paper "The Pricing of Options and Corporate Liabilities," trade in options has been booming. The most important functions of the option are risk management and arbitrage. Papers by Ross (1976), Breeden and Litzenberger (1978), and Arditti and Kose (1980) pointed out that the option spans opportunities which increase the efficiency of the financial market. Bookstaber and Clarke (1983, 1984) used the Monte Carlo simulation to test the influence the option has on the return distribution of the portfolio. Early studies in this area include Merton *et al.* (1978, 1982). But most of these research works focused on the equity option when spanning market opportunities. However, since 1973, after Fish Black and Myron Scholes created the model to price options, it is mainly used for arbitrage and risk management. In 2002 in Hong Kong market these two parts accounted for 41 percent and 46 percent of all trade in options.

Based on this, it is very important to gain insights into the complex option strategies used for arbitrage. Many books have been written to illustrate the characteristics of option strategies (Lin, 2010). However, only the method to construct these strategies is not enough for investors. Joshua and Tyler (2001) analyzed the return of strategies of single call, put, and zero-delta straddle in detail by using the data of S&P 500 in their paper "Expected option return." They analyzed the ERs by dividing them on the basis of different strike prices, at-the-money and out-of-the-money. They also used the results to derive the return's sensitivity to different parameters such as volatility, risk-free interest rate, and so on. It is very helpful for investors to learn about the characteristics of these kinds of strategies and it makes sense when trading in reality.

This chapter uses the criteria of ER, VaR, and CVaR to gain new insights into option strategies constructed for a single position, two positions, and even three or four positions. ER is the profit the investor is expected to earn. VaR and CVaR are important criteria for evaluating the potential risk the investor may bear. Ahn *et al.* (1997) once used VaR to evaluate the performance when using the option in risk management in their working paper "Optimal Risk Management Using Options."

Though using the option for arbitrage has been very popular and its share in financial markets has been growing, almost all financial organs design their strategies empirically. In reality, investors trust their experience more than quantitative analysis. In this context, the research in this chapter is very significant. The results can be used as a guide when investors use different options to construct the portfolio and it can help pre-calculate the risk and construct the portfolio such that risk stays within a certain range.

This chapter uses the option of the HSI as an example. The predicting data in this chapter is the result of a distortion of Monte Carlo simulation. Using the Monte Carlo simulation simulates the movement of the HSI, and then chooses at-the-money options to construct the different strategies. Any strategy so formulated can be ranked by different criteria such as ER, VaR and CVaR; strategies with a good performance can be chosen.

This chapter is composed of four main parts. The first and the second part are the introduction, which outlines the background, describes previous research works in the related field and the significance of analyzing the performance of different strategies. The third part is the model and the process to compare the different strategies. In the last part, the result is discussed and conclusions are drawn, besides summarizing the significance of this chapter and the meaning of the model proposed in this chapter.

8.3 Theoretical background and model

The model proposed in this chapter is based on the HSI, implying that the option strategies yielding a profit depend on the trend of the HSI. It is a European-style option which has an expiration date T and it can only be executed at the expiration date, though it can be traded at the market as a kind of merchandise. It has been mentioned that investors who use option strategies for arbitrage usually try to find the option which strays away from its normal value and earn the difference in value by buying and selling the option. There are dozens of option strategies which can be used for arbitrage and it is impossible to list all in one paper. However, according to one criterion, any kind of strategy can be chosen.

To evaluate the performance of these kinds of strategies, the movement of the HSI needs to be simulated. The most commonly used method is the Monte Carlo simulation. Based on the simulated movement of the HSI, at-the-money index options can be chosen to construct different strategies, such as call and put, which are single position, bull, bear, straddle, and strangle. Both these and butterfly and condor strategies involve two positions. The return of these strategies is based on the result of the simulation, so a one time simulation is not enough to analyze the regular pattern of these kinds of strategies. So different starting times are chosen for experiments and each experiment is iterated hundreds of times to calculate the return and risk of different strategies.

First, we choose the classical Monte Carlo simulation which is usually used in the financial area:

$$\frac{dS_t}{S_t} = \mu dt + \sigma dz_t \tag{8.1}$$

In this equation, S_t is the price of the underlying asset at time t and μ is the mean drift value while σ is the volatility and z_t is the geometric Brownian motion. As to the problem in this chapter, S_t can be viewed as the HSI, μ can use the value of risk free rate γ, and σ can be replaced by volatility of the HSI. Then by using this equation, we can simulate the movement of the HSI. The results of simulation are used to test the performance of index option strategies. Eight kinds of strategies are analyzed in this chapter, call, put, bull, bear, straddle, strangle, butterfly, and condor.

By using the simulation results, all of these strategies can be applied in virtual trading. The parameters of expected return (ER), VaR, and CVaR can be calculated to evaluate the performance of these strategies in this kind of virtual trading. The price of the index option in these simulations can be calculated by applying the Black–Scholes (BS) model, which is the classical option pricing model in both reality and theoretically. The equation of Black–Scholes used to calculate the price of index option can be expressed as:

$$[p_c^{t'}, p_p^{t'}] = blsprice(S_{t'}, K, r.T - t'.v, y) \tag{8.2}$$

where parameters $p_c^{t'}$ and $p_p^{t'}$ are prices of the corresponding call and put options at time t' and the corresponding value of the underlying asset is $S_{t'}$. The strike price is K and the time to maturity is T. r and v are the corresponding risk-free interest rate and volatility, respectively. y is annualized, continuously compounded yield of the underlying asset over the life of the option, expressed as a decimal number. In this chapter the default number is zero.

Trading is simulated by combining the Monte Carlo simulation and the BS model. As to the index options of the HSI traded in Hong Kong, only at-the-money options have the price and their liquidity is adequate for arbitrage. As to out-of-the-money options, prices are generally not available in reality. Even there are price quotes, liquidity is inadequate for arbitrage and it is hard for the investors to liquidate positions. Adding this kind of option leads to results far from real performance. To follow reality, strike prices of only around eight percent of the HSI options are selected for the simulation. This can cover almost all the volume of the Hang Seng market. Then to evaluate the performance of the strategies mentioned above, expected return, VaR, and CVaR need to be calculated for each round of simulation.

$$ER = \left(\sum_{n=1}^{N} \left(V_{t'}\left(S_{t'}^{n}, K, t'\right) - V_t\left(S_t^{n}, K, t\right)\right) \right) / N$$

$$VaR = V_{t'}\left(S_{t'} \bullet \theta(\alpha), K, t'\right) - V_t\left(S_t \bullet \theta(\alpha), K, t\right) \tag{8.3}$$

$$CVaR = V_{t'}\left(\beta\left(S_{t'} \bullet \theta(\alpha)\right), K, t'\right) - V_t\left(\beta\left(S_t \bullet \theta(\alpha)\right), K, t\right)$$

In these equations, N means the number of iterations of Monte Carlo simulation and K is the strike price. For strategies comprising more than one position, K is a vector. $\Delta t = t' - t$ is the holding period where t is the time to build the position while t' is the time to stop the position. The function V is used to calculate the value of the position. The function $\theta(\alpha)$ is a mapping function that follows the definition of VaR with boundary α. This boundary can find the corresponding value of the underlying asset for the specific strategies and for those the probability of which leading to the biggest loss not exceed $1-\alpha$. β is a cumulative function that follows the definition of CVaR. The function of β is a weighted average of VaR and losses exceeding the VaR. So CVaR is usually less or equal to the value of VaR. In this chapter probability α is defined as five percent.

The eight strategies mentioned above are calculated and they cover almost all normally used types of strategies. These eight strategies include one-position strategies such as single call or put and two-positions strategies such as bull, bear, straddle, and strangle, and even three- and four-positions strategies such as butterfly and condor. These strategies also cover upward and downward trends and fluctuation.

8.4 Results and analysis

In this section trading can be simulated and the results are analyzed in this part. Two experiments were conducted and 16 strategies were chosen for analysis: long call, short call, long put, short put, bull call, bull put, bear call, bear put, long straddle, short straddle, long strangle, short strangle, long butterfly, short butterfly, long condor, and short condor. These strategies are numbered one to 16.

Two experiments were done, the first from 12 December 2011 and the second from 12 February 2012. The time periods of the two experiments are both 100 days. For each of these two experiments, the Monte Carlo simulation was iterated 100 times. Figure 8.1 shows the mean value of the HSI of these two experiments; the dashed line is the trend of the first experiment started on 12 December 2011 while the real line is for the second experiment. The ordinate axis is the HSI and the cross shaft is the date. Compared with the first trend, the second line has an obvious trend in the next 100 days. This means the second experiment has higher volatility. These two experiments include both the fluctuant market and the clear trend market.

The two experiments have the same process and model; parameters and results are different. By doing the simulation, a series of distributions of the HSI can be obtained and then based on the distribution, the price of the index option can be calculated and the price is also a distribution. By comparing with the price on the starting day, the return of each strategy can be calculated. As to strategies with more than one position, all kinds of combinations are calculated. The performance of each strategy can be evaluated.

To evaluate these strategies, three kinds of criteria are selected, ER, VaR, and CVaR. The variances corresponding to these criteria also can be calculated to test the stability of these strategies.

The results are shown in tables in the Appendix. The first table is the result corresponding to 12 December 2011 while the second table corresponds to

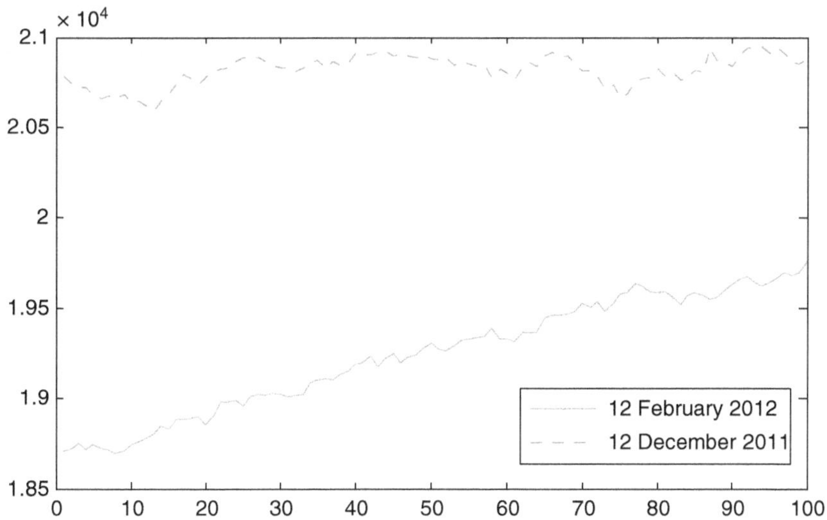

Figure 8.1 The mean value of Monte Carlo simulation.

12 February 2012. The two tables have the same contractures. The 16 columns represent these 16 strategies in the order we have mentioned above. Both of these two tables have six rows, and the first, third, and fifth row represent the ER, VaR, and CVaR while even numbered rows are variances corresponding to ER, VaR, and CVaR.

To analyze the performance intuitive from parameters of ER, ER's variance, the VaR, and the VaR's variance of these 16 strategies are shown in Figures 8.4 and 8.5. We will also carry out some analysis based on the results which are shown in these figures. Because the results of CVaR are very similar to the results of VaR, the data can be found in the Appendix. So it will not be analyzed in this part.

Figure 8.2 shows the expected return of these strategies in these two experiments. The horizontal axis from one to 16 represents the 16 strategies and the order corresponds to the order we mentioned above. In this figure, the dashed line represents the first experiment while the solid line represents the second.

Figure 8.2 keeps in accordance with the reality very well where the big win and the big loss always happens when there is a big trend in index. The odd number strategies and the even number strategies are usually opposed.

Of the 16 strategies, the first four usually have big gain or big loss when there is an obvious trend in the index because there is only one position. Straddle and strangle have the same characteristics with the single position but the swing is a little smaller than the single position strategies. Strategies such as bull call, bull put, bear call, bear put, butterfly, and condor usually have small swings. These characteristics can also be obtained from Figure 8.3, the variance of expected return of these 16 strategies.

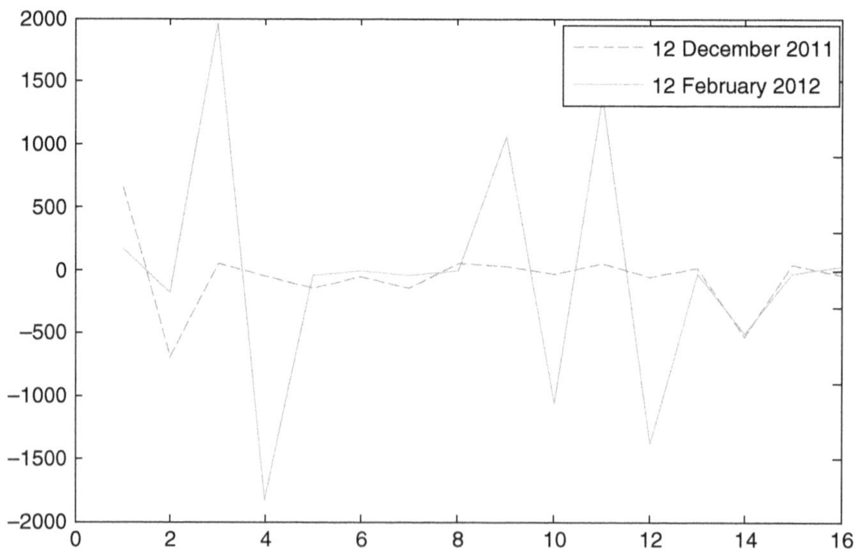

Figure 8.2 The mean expected return of these 16 strategies.

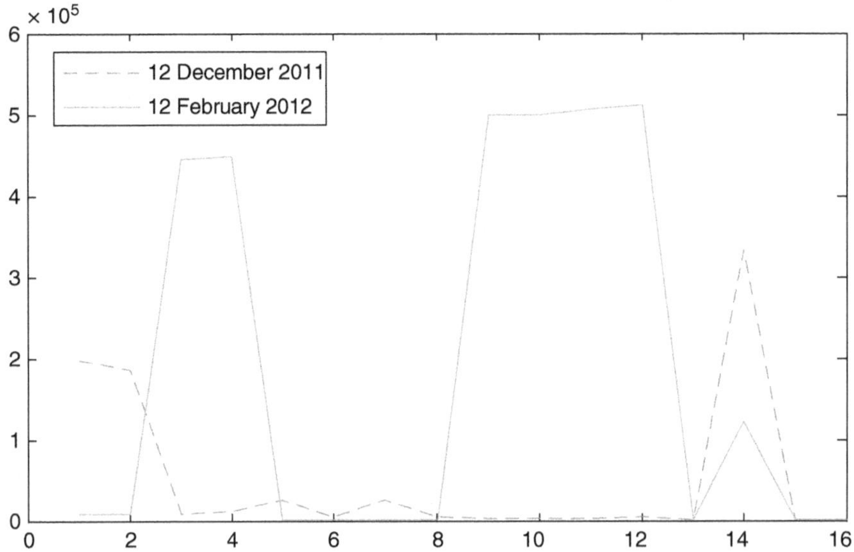

Figure 8.3 The variance of expected return of these 16 strategies.

From Figure 8.3, we can conclude that a return to bull, bear, butterfly, and condor usually has a lower variance, especially when the market has an obvious trend. But straddle, strangle, and strategies which have only one position show huge variances. This means these kinds of strategies bring high profits with high risk. A similar conclusion can be obtained from the analysis of VaR and CVaR also. It seems these kinds of strategies can resist the risk on their own to a certain degree, especially in a big market. So in this chapter, this performance can be viewed as a function of self-risk management. These kinds of strategies may not bring huge profits in one transaction and they also do not lead to huge losses. So if investors don't have much confidence in the future of the market, they may be a good choice. This provides a good chance for the risk averse to invest in the index option.

Figures 8.4 and 8.5, which are similar to the two above, also lead to similar conclusions, but represent VaR. As to the results of CVaR, because it is very similar to the result of VaR, we will not analyze the CVaR singly and only give the results in the Appendix.

Figure 8.4 shows the mean value of VaR of these strategies while Figure 8.5 gives the variance of the value of VaR. The same as the conclusion above, strategies of bull and bear can hold the risk well and the variance of VaR of these strategies is also small. This means even when the market has a huge fluctuation, the performance of these strategies is stable. But the difference is that though the strategies of butterfly and condor also have the characteristic of self-risk management, they don't perform well in the criteria VaR and CVaR. Since these two kinds of strategies don't perform well when the market has a big trend and fluctuation, we guess that this kind of strategy has many positions and these positions accumulate the risk which makes the VaR and CVaR not perform well.

So in conclusion, the single position strategies of index option are high risk, high return. The strategies of straddle and strangle have the same characteristics as the single position strategies. The strategies of bull and bear yield stable performance when the market has an obvious trend and when it fluctuates. The return is stable and they also can control the risk well. In the case of butterfly and condor, the expected return is stable but they still have higher risk inherent in situations with many positions.

The research described in this chapter includes almost all index strategies which are usually used in reality. The research covers strategies comprising one to four positions. What's more, the two experiments in this chapter are different; while one is the market with an obvious trend and the other one is fluctuation. It analyzes the functions of different strategies in self-risk management. Three criteria are chosen to analyze these strategies. The expected return represents the ability of these strategies to yield profit while VaR and CVaR are used to measure the risk the investor faces.

The disadvantages are that the option data are from the Hang Seng market, so the results are suitable only for the Hong Kong market. Because of the constraint of time required to calculate the price of option by using the BS model, the number of repetitions of the Monte Carlo simulation is not enough to get more information and to get more accurate results. The other aspect of the disadvantages is that the

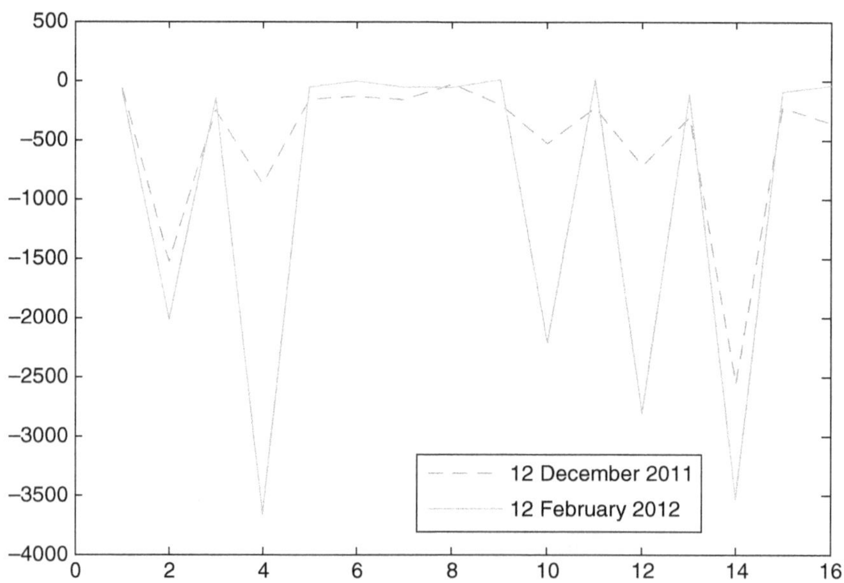

Figure 8.4 The VaR of these 16 strategies.

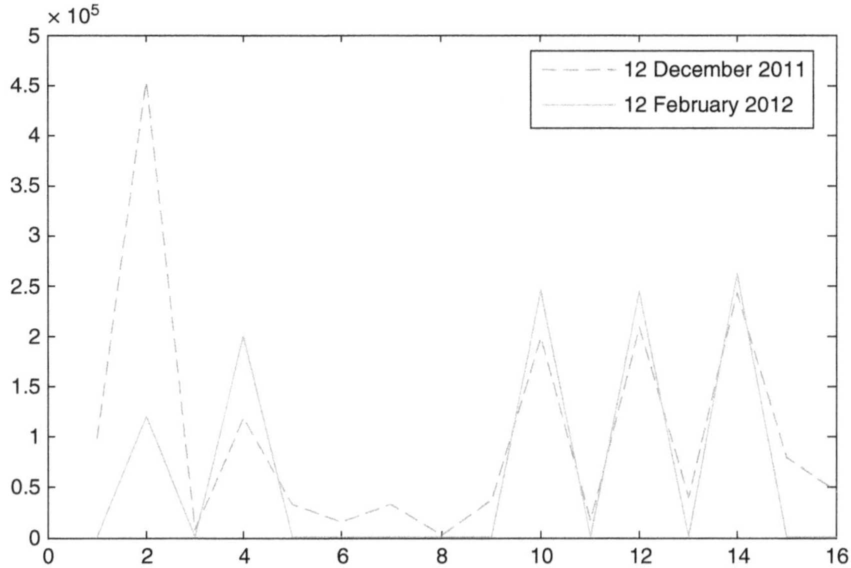

Figure 8.5 The variance of VaR of these 16 strategies.

value of index option is calculated by using the BS model, so it is impossible to avoid mispricing of the model against reality. What's more, this chapter only gives the characteristics and the rules of these strategies. It doesn't give recommendations to the investors. Maybe in the future, if there is a method which can predict the index distribution by combining the methods in this chapter, recommendations can be made to the investors.

8.5 Conclusions

This chapter is the first to analyze index option strategies characteristics quantitatively, using specific evaluation criteria, to support investors for gaining insights and formulating strategies when using options for arbitrage. By using the Monte Carlo simulation to calculate the distribution of the HSI, the statistical results are calculated. The results state that the single position strategies of index option are high risk, high return. The strategies of straddle and strangle have the same characteristics as single position strategies.

Bull and bear strategies perform in a stable manner when the market has an obvious trend as well as when it experiences fluctuations. The return is stable and they also can control the risk well. Butterfly and condor also provide stable expected returns but they have the higher risk inherent in multiple positions. Quantified results are given in the Appendix. It is helpful for the investors because it not only analyses the expected return but also the ability for risk management.

Because of the difficulty in hedging the risk of the index option, the self-risk management is very important for investors who are risk averse. What's more the expected return and the risk of the strategies are the most important to investors. So making new insights and analyzing the index strategies quantitatively have great significance for trading in index options. So this chapter makes sense both in theoretical circles and real trading.

Appendix

Table 8.1 Mean value of expected return, VaR, CVaR and the variance of these three criteria based on the Monte Carlo simulation from 12 December 2011 for the following 100 days

	Long call	*Short call*	*Long put*	*Short put*	*Bull call*	*Bull put*	*Bear call*	*Bear put*
ER	658.831	−698.781	52.71546	−43.9642	−143.499	−53.1794	−145.882	54.10272
R-variance	19669.94	18500.73	837.3808	1140.378	2607.711	422.526	2616.245	426.2803
VaR	−70.993	−1530.15	−258.43	−875.565	−164.849	−141.58	−164.849	−26.4358
VaR-variance	981.8183	454.9192	85.93595	1197.329	321.5089	154.6704	321.5089	156.0981
CVaR	−135.013	−1851.65	−276.431	−1258.41	−166.779	−148.774	−166.779	−37.7429
CVaR-variance	825.2752	4923.256	93.21392	2331.905	330.8407	176.7933	330.8407	17.37526
	Long straddle	*Short straddle*	*Long strangle*	*Short strangle*	*Long butterfly*	*Short butterfly*	*Long condor*	*Short condor*
ER	31.65849	−31.6585	49.05539	−52.3391	17.77206	−531.9	36.06751	−36.2274
ER-variance	196.8721	196.8721	273.2593	373.1577	16.80448	33292.8	76.644	77.39374
VaR	−208.246	−532.709	−223.775	−723.497	−304.954	−2558.18	−236.142	−364.798
VaR-variance	372.0767	2000.059	171.6522	2098.453	404.6398	2433.08	801.9038	458.2672
CVaR	−213.066	−742.999	−228.067	−1037.08	−316.512	−3180.8	−250.113	−375.673
CVaR-variance	390.6867	3820.679	17.4402	4251.459	429.8912	4042.206	870.9459	429.2435

Table 8.2 Mean value of expected return, VaR, CVaR and the variance of these three criteria based on the Monte Carlo simulation from 12 February 2012 for the following 100 days

	Long call	*Short call*	*Long put*	*Short put*	*Bull call*	*Bull put*	*Bear call*	*Bear put*
ER	163.9715	−186.518	1959.297	−1825.41	−46.0866	−1.17287	−46.1293	−4.89665
R-variance	8342.47	8461.278	444741.1	447715.3	793.0253	122.4277	795.3619	89.22017
VaR	−97.7712	−2023.96	−145.267	−3658.01	−64.211	−11.6422	−64.211	−59.4784
VaR-variance	193.8093	120935.2	302.199	201222.7	164.2511	9.652918	164.2511	100.9211
CVaR	−98.5935	−4463.02	−154.342	−3749.57	−65.9956	−13.5177	−65.9956	−64.1349
CVaR-variance	196.9691	347033.8	327.0306	215251.6	172.0292	10.88545	172.0292	110.2686
	Long straddle	*Short straddle*	*Long strangle*	*Short strangle*	*Long butterfly*	*Short butterfly*	*Long condor*	*Short condor*
ER	1057.809	−1057.81	1387.095	−1391.27	−28.6959	−509.269	−34.9971	34.99712
ER-variance	498475.9	498475.9	506241.1	510973.7	415.6132	121679.3	679.32	679.32
VaR	12.3788	−2218.64	3.530885	−2807.49	−116.928	−3536.58	−104.63	−48.9318
VaR-variance	68.77803	245925.9	55.07265	245513	266.8005	261963.5	235.7471	73.69592
CVaR	−20.759	−2789.16	−29.7795	−3541.12	−123.059	−4599.37	−110.219	−60.8307
CVaR-variance	47.29136	396438.6	41.79015	395429.3	293.6506	441731.4	257.7949	88.73688

9 Call–put term structure spread-based Hang Seng Index analysis

The Hang Seng Volatility Index (VHSI) measures the 30-calendar-day expected volatility of the Hang Seng Index (HSI). It is derived from HSI put options and HSI call options in the two nearest-term expiration months in order to bracket a 30-calendar-day period. Long-term and regular trends of the HSI and the VHSI have intensive negative correlation and the VHSI is calculated from the implied volatility of out-of-the-money option which means the implied volatility of call and put options can reflect some information of the trend of the HSI. Usually, call and put options have different performances when the HSI goes upwards and downwards. So if the volatilities can be calculated separately and then the different changes of call–put spread are analyzed, it may form a good indicator of movement of the HSI. Based on these theories, this chapter describes calculation of the implied volatility of call and put options separately. The curves of implied volatilities of both call and put can be drawn and the distance between them, which is called "call–put spread" can be calculated.

9.1 Introduction

The methodology of the VHSI is based on the CBOE Volatility Index (VIX) in the US market. Modifications have been made to take into account trading characteristics of HSI options in the Hong Kong market. For each of the near-term and next-term options, out-of-the-money call options with strike prices lower than or equal to 120 percent of at-the-money strike price are selected. Out-of-the-money put options with strike prices higher than or equal to 80 percent of the at-the-money strike price are selected. The methodology has been published by Hang Seng Bank. According to long-term observations, the trend of the VHSI has a significant negative correlation with the trend of the HSI, and this result has been generally accepted by the industry. That means the VHSI contains much information which has a relationship with the HSI. According to a statement of the Hang Seng Bank, the VHSI is calculated by combining implied volatility of call and put options. So the implied volatility of options can reflect the movement of the HSI. Andersen *et al.* have done the related work that examines forward-looking market-based implied volatility in 2003. We know that call options and put options have different behaviors when the HSI goes upwards or downwards. Inspired by this result, this chapter tries to calculate and combine the implied volatility of call and put options, and by analyzing the spread between the call volatility and put volatility to predict the trend of the HSI. The implied volatility of call and put options is calculated by using the mainstream Black–Scholes (B–M) model, which is widely used in financial engineering.

By using the BS model, once the parameters of price (underlying asset), strike price, rate, time to maturity, value of the option, and the style (call or put) are known, implied volatility can be calculated. Implied volatility, a forward-looking measure, differs from historical volatility because the latter is calculated from known past returns of a security. Because of the importance of implied volatility, many scholars have done related work to provide insights into implied volatility and have made great contributions to the development of research in the field of implied volatility (Andersen *et al.*, 2003; Bollerslev and Zhou, 2002, 2003; Bollerslev *et al.*, 2007). Most of their works are focused on how to calculate the implied volatility accurately but not to use the information contained in implied volatility to predict the trend of the market. Standard deviations implied in option prices are used as predictors of future stock price variability (Beckers, 1981). Derman and Kani (1994a, b), Dupire (1994), and Rubinstein (1994) hypothesized that asset return volatility is a deterministic function of asset price and time and developed a deterministic volatility function (DVF) option valuation model that has the potential of fitting the observed cross section of option prices exactly. But it is no better than an *ad hoc* procedure that merely smooths the BS (Black and Scholes, 1973) implied volatilities across exercise prices and times to expiration (Dumas *et al.*, 1998). So, in this chapter the BS model is used to calculate the implied volatility and it is used as predictor of the trend of the HSI.

The idea mentioned above is based on the different performances of implied volatility of call and put options and the intensive negative relationship between the VHSI and the HSI. The VHSI is divided into volatilities of call and put options and then both call and put options are divided into different groups by expiration date. Because there are almost no option deals which have a long time to maturity, only options due to expire within a few months are selected. The mean values of the same style options which have the same expiry dates can be calculated. Then two curves can be drawn. The first is the curve of the mean value of implied volatility of call options while the second one is put options. These two curves always change with movement of the HSI. There is a lot of information in these two curves, especially the interspace and the relative positions of them. When there is a downward trend in the market, implied volatility of put options is usually higher while in an upward trend, implied volatility of call options is higher. So we try to build the model to test the relationship between implied volatility and the trend of HSI. Then the spread between the implied volatility curve of call and put options is calculated as the indicator to predict the trend of the market. In this chapter, the HSI options are chosen to calculate these two curves and the time period is 15 minutes. That means every 15 minutes all data of options which have volume are calculated to predict the trend of the next 15 minutes. The data of one year, from April 2011 to April 2012, are selected to build the model to predict the trend of the HSI.

This chapter is composed of four main parts. The first part is the introduction which outlines the background, describes previous research works in related field and the reason to do research about this field. The second part is the theoretical background and technology used in the model and the process of prediction. In the third part, the result is given to prove the efficiency of the model in predicting the HSI. In the last part, the results are discussed and conclusions are drawn, besides summarizing the significance of this chapter and the meaning of the model proposed in this chapter is explained.

9.2 Theoretical background and model

9.2.1 Data

The data in this chapter were collected from the Hong Kong market from April 2011 to April 2012. The time period is 15 minutes, which means the data are collected from the market every 15 minutes and data of options which have prices in the 15 minutes are collected, including the value of the options, style, expired date and so on. The risk free rate, which corresponds to the interest rate and the corresponding HSI used to test the efficiency of the model are all real data of Hong Kong market. As we have mentioned above, once the parameters of price (underlying asset), strike price, rate, time to maturity, value of the options, and the style (call or put) are known, the implied volatility can be calculated using the BS model. Based on the data we collect, the implied volatility of each option which has a price can be calculated and these volatilities are the input parameters for the prediction model.

9.2.2 Theoretical background

The initial data are used for calculating the corresponding volatilities. Berestycki *et al.* (2004) stated the method to calculate the implied volatility in their paper "Computing the Implied Volatility in Stochastic Volatility Models." Many scholars have done a lot of work in the field of implied volatility (Lee, 2004; Shehata and Mickaiel, 2012). As is known and mentioned above, the BS model is the mainstream option pricing model and any one of the parameters can be calculated once the other parameters are known. So the equation to calculate the implied volatility can be written as:

$$IV = blsiv(P, S, r, T - t, v, y, B) \tag{9.1}$$

In this equation, IV is implied volatility to be calculated, and $blsiv(\bullet)$ is the BS function used to calculate IV. The parameter P is the price of the underlying asset. The HSI option is expressed as "HSI." S is the strike price of the corresponding option. T is the expired date while t is the time now. Then the meaning of parameter $T - t$ is the time to maturity. v is the value of the corresponding option and

y is annualized, continuously compounded yield of the underlying asset. Here the default value for y is zero. B is a binary parameter, call or put, which states the style of the option.

VHSI, which is known as a combination of implied volatilities of out-of-the-money call options and put options has an intensive negative relationship with the HSI. It proves that implied volatility contains information of the trend of the HSI. But we know that implied volatilities of call options and put options usually have different changes whenever the Hong Kong market goes upwards or downwards. So, if we can divide the implied volatilities of call options and put options into two curves and analyze the relationship between these two curves, it may be a good indicator for prediction of the HSI. By using the theory of the BS model to calculate the implied volatility and inspired by the VHSI and the different performances of call and put options, the model using implied volatility to predict the trend of the HSI is built in the next part.

9.2.3 Model

The model can be divided into two parts. The first part is calculating the implied volatility of options and drawing the curves of implied volatility of call options and put options separately; the second is to use the information contained in these two curves to predict the trend of the HSI.

As to the first part, parameters of all options trades in the Hong Kong market, for the period from April 2011 to April 2012 are collected, in intervals of 15 minutes. There are in total 5,398 records for the whole year. The equation of the BS model is defined in (9.1).

Implied volatilities of the nearest five expired dates options which have pricing can be calculated using equation (9.1), because there are almost no records for options whose expired dates are too far away.

Then, the same style options have the same expired date:

$$IV_B^{T_i} = \sum_{j=1}^{N} \beta_{B_j} IV_{B_j}^{T_i} / N \quad (i = 1, 2, 3, 4, 5 \quad B = call\ or\ put) \tag{9.2}$$

where β_{B_j} is the weight of implied volatility of jth with style B. Because of the different style or the different strike price, contribution the implied volatility can make is usually different. So it is necessary to give them a weight.

By using the equations above, all 5,398 records are chosen. For each record, we can draw figures like Figures 9.1 and 9.2.

Then by adding these two figures into one, we can find that there are changes in the implied volatility of both call and put options.

As mentioned above, curves of implied volatilities of call options and put options change with time. The single picture can represent the state of the market at one point, as shown in Figures 9.1 and 9.2. Intuitively, we know that if there is a high value of the VHSI, it means investors are panicky and worry about the fall of the market. The same is the case with the model in this chapter. If we put the two consecutive figures together, it is better for us to analyze the changes of the panic situation. The distance, such as distance 1 and distance 2 marked on Figure 9.3, is called the call–put spread in this chapter. Now the first part of the model, calculating the two curves of implied volatility of call options and put options, is completed. In the following, we complete the second part which has been mentioned in the first part. That is, we use the call–put spread to build the model to predict the trend of the HSI.

Using Equations (9.1) and (9.2), we get Figures 9.1, 9.2, and 9.3. The space between the curve of put options and the curve of call options is called the spread which can be abstracted as the distance marked on Figure 9.3. Then using distance 1 and 2 in Figure 9.3 as examples, they can be written as

$$\begin{cases} \text{distance } 1 = D_{5398}^{T_2} = IV_{C_{5398}}^{T_2} - IV_{P_{5398}}^{T_2} \\ \text{distance } 2 = D_{5378}^{T_3} = IV_{C_{5378}}^{T_3} - IV_{P_{5378}}^{T_3} \end{cases} \tag{9.3}$$

In reality, the relationship between the call–put spread and the HSI is complex. It is difficult to use an equation to quantify this kind of relationship. So the model in this chapter, instead of making quantitative prediction of the HSI, makes only qualitative prediction, by using the call put spread.

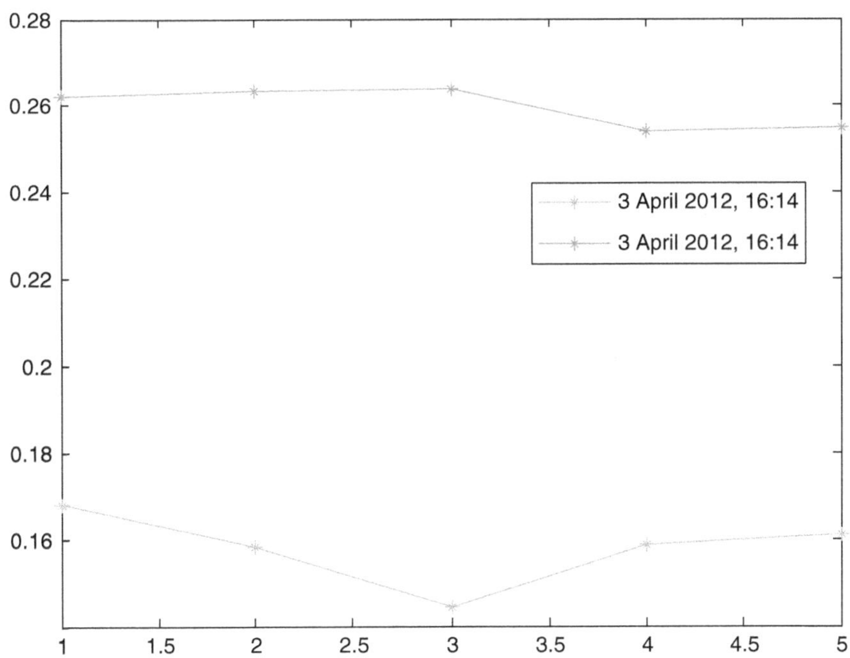

Figure 9.1 The implied volatility of 3 April 2012, 16:14.

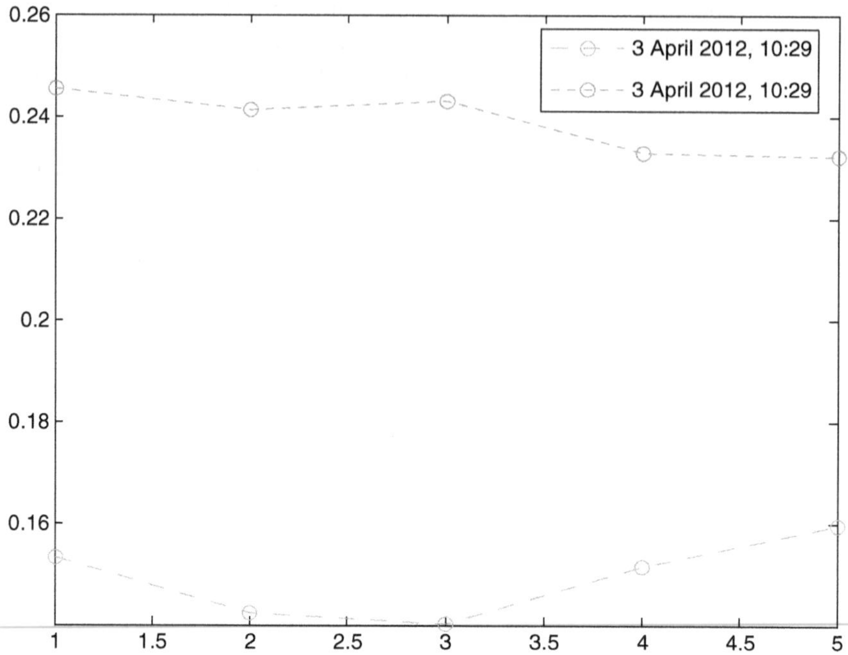

Figure 9.2 The implied volatility of 3 April 2012, 10:29.

The mean level, IVC_t, of the implied volatility of call option at time t in Figure 9.4 can be written as

$$IVC_t = \sum_{i=1}^{5} IV_{C_t}^{T_i}/5 \tag{9.4}$$

IVC_t is the level which is the mean value of implied volatility of call options with different expired dates at time t. Parameter $IV_{C_t}^{T_i}$ can by calculated by Equation (9.2). In the same way, the level of implied volatility of put options at time t can be written as

$$IVP_t = \sum_{i=1}^{5} IV_{P_t}^{T_i}/5 \tag{9.5}$$

Equation (9.5) has the same meaning as Equation (9.4). By using Equations (9.4) and (9.5), Figure 9.4 can be drawn. The parameter in Figure 9.5 can be written as

$$DIF_t = IVC_t - IVP_t \tag{9.6}$$

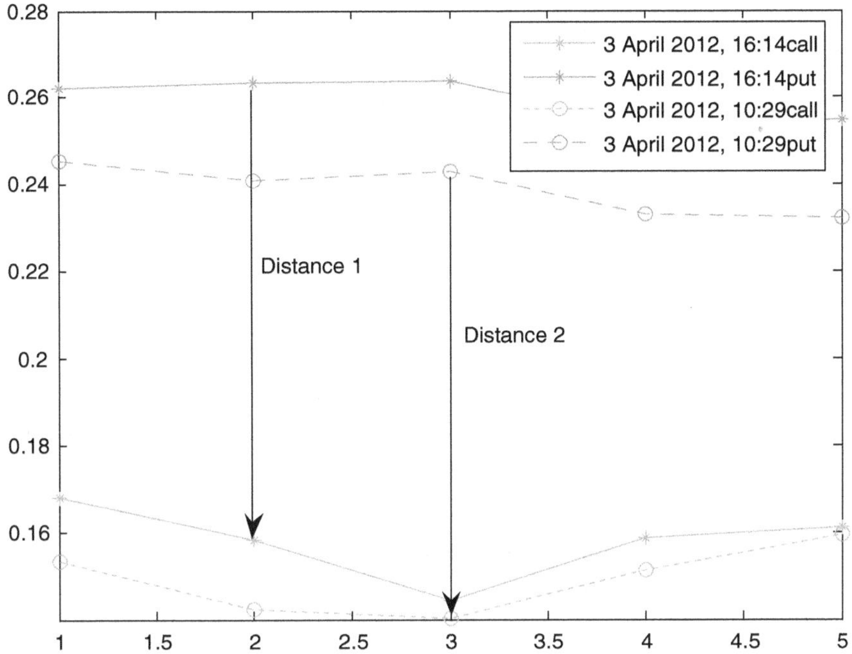

Figure 9.3 The implied volatility of 3 April 2012, 16:14 and 3 April 2012, 10:29.

Based on the theory of implied volatility and the characteristics of implied volatility of call and put options, the model can be abstracted as the judgment of the changing of DIF_t and it can be written as

$$\begin{cases} DIF_{t+1} - DIF_t \geq 0 \Rightarrow HSI_{t+2} - HSI_{t+1} \geq 0 \\ DIF_{t+1} - DIF_t \leq 0 \Rightarrow HSI_{t+2} - HSI_{t+1} \leq 0 \end{cases} \quad t \geq 0 \tag{9.7}$$

Then this model can use the two previous time periods to predict the trend of the HSI in the following time period.

The model illustrated above is the basic model created in this chapter. Because most scholars think the near term option can reflect the near term trend of the HSI better, the predicting model which uses the nearest expired date options is treated as the benchmark. Then Equation (9.7) can be rewritten as

$$\begin{cases} DIF_{t+1}^{T_1} - DIF_t^{T_1} \geq 0 \Rightarrow HSI_{t+2} - HSI_{t+1} \geq 0 \\ DIF_{t+1}^{T_1} - DIF_t^{T_1} \leq 0 \Rightarrow HSI_{t+2} - HSI_{t+1} \leq 0 \end{cases} \quad t \geq 0 \tag{9.8}$$

where parameter $DIF_{t+1}^{T_1}$ is not the mean value of five expired dates options. It is implied volatility of only the nearest expired date option and the equation is written as

$$DIF_{t+1}^{T_1} = IV_{C_t}^{T_1} - IV_{P_t}^{T_1} \tag{9.9}$$

In fact, whether the expiry date of an option is near or far, implied volatility of both contains information of the trend of the index. Both can be used as the indicator of the HSI to a certain degree, though they may have different weights. So the prediction model with weight should have a better performance in theory. Then compared with the mean weight model Equations (9.4) and (9.5) can be rewritten as

$$IVC_t = \frac{\sum_{i=1}^{5} \beta_i \cdot IV_{C_t}^{T_i}}{\sum_{i=1}^{5} \beta_i} \quad \text{and} \quad IVP_t = \frac{\sum_{i=1}^{5} \beta_i \cdot IV_{P_t}^{T_i}}{\sum_{i=1}^{5} \beta_i} \tag{9.10}$$

β_i denotes the weight assigned to different volatilities of different expiry dates options. It is necessary to find the optimal value of β_i. In theory, β_i should be bigger than or equal to β_{i+1}.

In the following part, we give the analysis about the rationality of the model and analyze the results of these three models. The advantages and disadvantages are also analyzed and some directions are suggested for future research.

9.3 Results and analysis

Figure 9.4 clearly depicts the relationship between the HSI and the mean value of volatilities of call and put options, and Figure 9.5 shows the relationship between the difference in volatilities of call and put options and the HSI and the time interval in both is 15 minutes.

From Figure 9.4, it is obvious that before the point of 3,000, there is a downward trend in the HSI and during this time period, parameter *IVP* is bigger than parameter *IVC*. Between the point of 3,000 and 6,000, there is an upward trend in the HSI. As to this time period, in most cases the level of volatility of call options is a little higher than that of put options. What's more, when there is intense turbulence in the market, the spread between volatility of call options and put options is bigger than usual. This characteristic will be helpful for future work which may focus on quantitative predictions.

In Figure 9.5, the solid line is the HSI corresponding to the line in Figure 9.4 and it is the value of the HSI. The conclusion is shown in Figure 9.5; when there is a downward trend, the value of parameter DIF_t is lower and vice versa.

Based on the analysis to these two figures, it is clear that the conclusion assumed above is rational. Results in Table 9.1 also prove the efficiency of the model in predicting the trend of the HSI.

Table 9.1 shows the result of the three models in this chapter. There is no big difference between these three models. But we still can conclude that the weighted model perform best while the nearest model is the worst which is accordant to the hypothesis we made. Values of parameters in the weighted model are $\beta_1 = \beta_2 =$

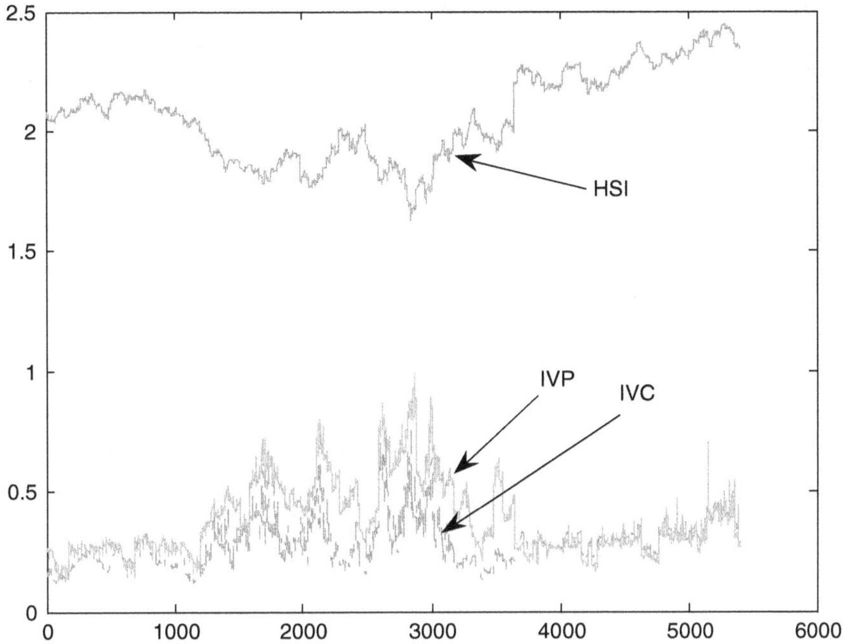

Figure 9.4 The HSI, IVP, and IVC.

$\beta_3 = \beta_4 = 1$ which is bigger than $\beta_5 = 0.9$. The range of these parameters is from 0 to 1 and the step to search the best solution is 0.1. Because the step is a little long, the best solution may be skipped during the process of searching. So this must not be the best solution for the weighted model. If the step length can be reduced to 0.01, it will be more accurate for this model and better results can be obtained.

Results in the table and the two figures, Figure 9.4 and Figure 9.5, prove the efficiency of the model well. The conclusions are accordant with the hypothesis proposed in the former part of the article, that implied volatility of call and put options is a good indicator of the trend of the HSI and what's more, volatility of options with different expired dates have different weights to the function of predicting. However, all of these three models have no big difference while the hit rate and hit numbers are almost the same. The numbers they can rightly predict are all around 2,900 out of the 5,398 records from April 2011 to April 2012.

There are both advantages and disadvantages in these models. Here advantages and disadvantages of the weighted model, which is the most complete model among these three, are analyzed. The model is very simple and it is easy to calculate and to get values of the parameters. What's more, in predicting the trend of the HSI, it can always get stable results, around 54 percent. It is a significant benchmark for research in the future and it is a good result for trading in reality. Though it is a simple and useful model, it is not enough to mine all the information involved in the implied volatility of options. Better result can be got if the model is better. One shortcoming of this model is that the implied volatility for any given time period is the mean value of all options which are traded. This is not accurate, because of the existence of the volatility smile and a lot of work has been done in this field. The volatility of the deeply out-of-the-money option is always higher and the information in deeply out-of-the-money may be not accurate, so the method of calculating the mean value leads to an error while volatility of deeply out-of-the-money options has the same weight as the other options. The method to solve this problem is not difficult. Just take the volatility smile into account and assign only slight weights to deeply out-of-the-money options, to reduce their impact. So for future research, if the volatility smile can be taken into account, the results will be better.

The other shortcoming of the models in this chapter is that the prediction is qualitative, which means only the direction of the HSI can be predicted. Though it provides good results for trading in reality, quantitative prediction is perfect for trading. But compared with the qualitative prediction, quantitative prediction is much more difficult because the relationship between the delta of the HSI and the delta of volatility is very complex, even it may be not possible to express it in equations. But it is still a good direction for future research.

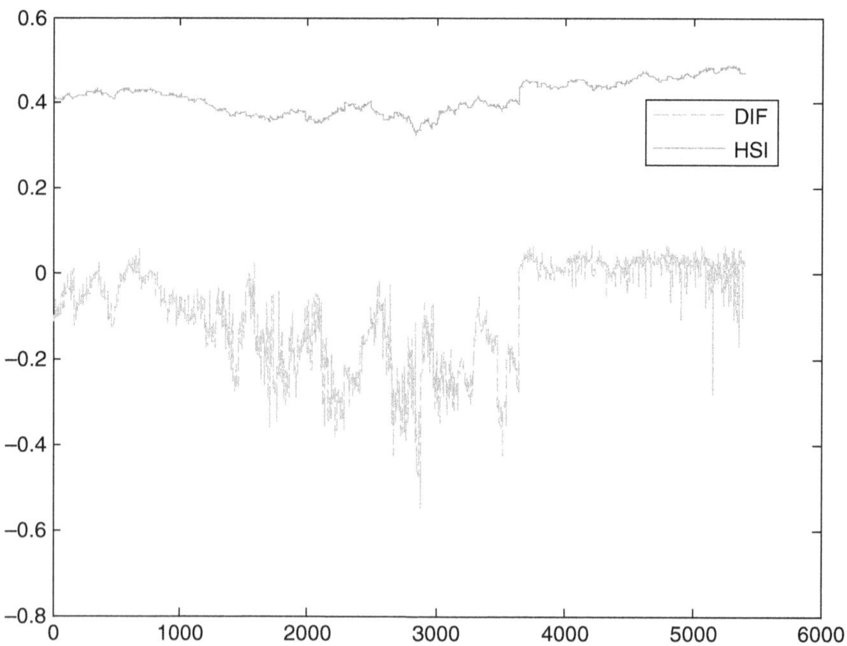

Figure 9.5 The HSI and DIF.

Table 9.1 The results of the prediction

	Mean	*Nearest*	*Weighted*
Hit rate	54.30%	53.48%	54.34%
Hit number	2,930	2,894	2,933

What's more, because of the limitation of the data in this research, the time interval is 15 minutes and the authors did not try any other time intervals. It may not be a good time interval for prediction of Hong Kong market. In future, other time intervals can be tested. This may lead to a good result too. In a word, though the research in this chapter is very significant and important, there still are shortcomings and a lot of work still can be done in the future to make the model complete and to make the prediction accurate.

9.4 Conclusions

Inspired by the intensive negative relationship between the VHSI and the HSI and the different performances of implied volatilities of put and call options, this is the first instance when the VHSI has been divided into volatilities of call options and volatility of put options and the changes of the position of these two volatilities, which means the call–put spread, is used as the indicator to predict the trend of the HSI. The call–put spread is complex and in this chapter it is abstracted from the distance between volatilities of call options and put options. It can make the model simple.

Three models, the nearest term volatility, the mean value, and the weighted volatilities model, have been constructed in this chapter to test the efficiency of the call–put spread in predicting the trend of the HSI. The method of using the call–put spread to predict the index of market is first stated in this chapter and the results show that the models are rational. This opens the direction to calculate volatilities of call and put options separately, which is different from the VHSI that combines them and it is also the first time the information contained in the position of volatilities of call and put options has been dug out. All of these three models have similar results, and the results in the last part show the correctness of these models and prove that there is a lot of information in the call–put spread.

Moreover, both advantages and disadvantages were analyzed in the former part and based on that analysis the author has shown the direction for future research. Though only qualitative prediction is made in this chapter, it opens a new direction for predicting the index. The possibility of making quantitative prediction is also given in the former part. It is a new topic for the research of volatility of options. The research in this chapter not only makes a significant contribution to the research area but also to trading in reality.

Notes

2 A novel model-free term structure for stock prediction

1 HIBOR is Hong Kong Interbank Offered Rate, the annualized offer rate that banks in Hong Kong offer for a specified period ranging from overnight to one year, normally including overnight, 1 week, 2 weeks, 1 month, 2 months, 3 months, 6 months, and 1 year.

2 In mathematics, a particular type of stochastic process applies Ito's Lemma to calculate the differential of a function. It is named after Kiyoshi Ito, who discovered the lemma. It is the counterpart of stochastic calculus in ordinary calculus. It uses the Taylor series expansion by conserving the second order term in calculus. This lemma is widely used in finance and related fields. It is best known for its application for deriving the BS option pricing model.

6 A novel mean reversion-based local volatility model

1 Since the local volatility is a function of underlying asset price and time and the time is assumed to be fixed, we will go through the proof of Y'_S with different prices S converging to its long-run mean level. This is the same process as underlying asset price is fixed as mentioned above. Therefore, we only discuss one case in this paper.

References

Ahn, Dong-Hyun, Jacob Boundoukh, Matthew Richardson and Robert F. Whitelaw (1997). Optimal Risk Management Using Options. *Working Paper of National Bureau of Economic Research.*

Andersen, G. Torben, Luca Benzoni and Jesper Lund (2002). An Empirical Investigation of Continuous-Time Equity Return Models. *Journal of Finance* **57**(3): 1239–1284.

Andersen, G. Torben, Tim Bollerslev and Francis X. Diebold (2003). *Handbook of Financial Econometrics*, chap. Parametric and Nonparametric Volatility Measurement. Elsevier Science: Mexico, USA.

Arditti, Fred D. and John Kose (1980). Spanning the State Space with Options. *Journal of Financial Quantitative Analysis* **15**: 1–9.

Asaia, Manabu and Michael McAleer (2009). The Structure of Dynamic Correlations in Multivariate Stochastic Volatility Models. *Journal of Econometrics* **150**(2): 182–92.

Bates, David S. (2000). Post-87 Crash Fears in S&P 500 Futures Options. *Journal of Econometrics* **94**: 181–238.

Beckers, Stan (1981). Standard Deviations Implied in Option Prices as Predictors of Future Stock Price Variability. *Journal of Banking and Finance* **5**(3): 363–81.

Benhamou, Eric, Emmanuel Gobet and Mohammed Miri (2010). Time dependent Heston model. *SIAM Journal on Financial Mathematics* **1**: 289–325.

Berestycki, Henri, Jerome Busca and Igor Florent (2004). Computing the Implied Volatility in Stochastic Volatility Models. *Communications on Pure and Applied Mathematics* **LVII**: 1352–73.

Bessembinder, Hendrik, Jay Coughenour, Paul Seguin and Margaret Monroe Smoller (1995). Mean Reversion in Equilibrium Asset Prices: Evidence from the Futures Term Structure. *Journal of Finance* **50**(1): 361–75.

Black, Fischer (1990). Mean Reversion and Consumption Smoothing. *Review of Financial Studies* **3**(1): 107–14.

Black, Fischer and Myron Scholes (1973). The Pricing of Options and Corporate Liabilities. *The Journal of Political Economy* **81**: 637–54.

Bollerslev, Tim and Hao Zhou (2002). Estimating Stochastic Volatility Diffusion Using Conditional Moments of Integrated Volatility. *Journal of Econometrics* **109**: 33–65.

Bollerslev, Tim and Hao Zhou (2003). Volatility Puzzles: A Unified framework for Gauging Return-Volatility Regressions. *Working Paper of National Bureau of Economic Research.*

Bollerslev, Tim, Michael Gibson and Hao Zhou (2007). Dynamic Estimation of Volatility Risk Premia and Investor Risk Aversion form Option-Implied and Realized Volatility. *Working Paper of National Bureau of Economic Research.*

Bookstaber, Richard and Roger Clarke (1983). An Algorithm to Calculate the Return Distribution of Portfolios with Option Positions. *Management Science* **29**(4): 419–29.

Bookstaber, Richard and Roger Clarke (1984). Option Portfolio Strategies: Measurement and Evaluation. *Journal of Business* **57**(4): 469–92.

Breeden, Douglas T. and Robert H. Litzenberger (1978). Price of State-contingent Claims Implicit in Option Price. *Journal of Business* **52**: 621–51.

Britten-Jones, Mark and Anthony Neuberger (2000). Option Prices, Implied Price Processes, and Stochastic Volatility. *Journal of Finance* **55**: 839–66.

Carr, Peter and Dilip Madan (2001). *Towards a Theory of Volatility Trading*. Chapter 12, pp. 458–76. Cambridge University Press: Cambridge, UK.

Carr, Peter and Liuren Wu (2009). Variance Risk Premiums. *Review of Financial Studies* **22**: 1311–41.

Cecchetti, Stephen, Pok-Sang Lam and Mark Nelson (1990). Mean Reversion in Equilibrium Asset Prices. *The American Economic Review* **80**(3): 398–418.

Chernov, Mikhail and Eric Ghysels (2000). A Study Towards a Unified Approach to the Joint Estimation of Objective and Risk Neutral Measures for the Purpose of Option Valuation. *Journal of Financial Economics* **56**: 407–58.

Christoffersen, Peter, Steve Heston and Kris Jacobs (2006). The Shape and Term Structure of the Index Option Smirk: Why Multifactor Stochastic Volatility Models Work so Well. *Management Science* **55**: 1914–32.

Coleman, Thomas, Yuying Li and Arun Verma (1999). Reconstructing the Unknown Local Volatility Function. *Journal of Computational Finance* **2**(3): 77–100.

Coval, Joshua D. and Shumway Tyler (2001). Expected Option Return. *The Journal of Finance* **56**(3): 983–1009.

Cox, John (1975). Notes on Option Pricing I: Constant Elasticity of Diffusions. *Working Paper of Stanford University, California*.

Crépey, Stéphane (2003). Calibration of the Local Volatility in a Generalized Black–Scholes Model using TIKHONOV Regularization. *SIAM Journal of Mathematical Analysis* **34**(5): 1183–206.

Demeterfi, Kresimir, Emanuel Derman, Michael Kamal and Joseph Zou (1999). A Guide to Volatility and Variance Swaps. *Journal of Derivatives* **6**(4): 9–32.

Derman, Emanuel and Iraj Kani (1997) "Stochastic implied trees: Arbitrage pricing with stochastic term and strike structure of volatility." Quantitative Strategies Technical Notes, Goldman Sachs.

Derman, Emanuel and Iraj Kani (1994b). Riding on the Smile. *Risk* **7**: 32–9.

Dumas, Bernard, Jeff Fleming and Robert E. Whaley (1998). Implied Volatility Functions: Empirical Tests. *Journal of Finance* **53**(6): 2059–106.

Dupire, Bruno (1994). Pricing with a Smile. *Risk* **7**: 18–20.

Emanuel, David and James MacBeth (1982). Further Results of the Constant Elasticity of Variance Call Option Pricing Model. *Journal of Financial and Quantitative Analysis* **4**: 533–53.

Engle, Robert and Andrew Patton (2001). What Good Is a Volatility Model? *Quantitative Finance* **1**: 237–45.

Ernst and Young (1999). Internet Shopping: An Ernst and Young Special Report. *Ernst and Young LLP*.

Feng, Jin, Martin Forde and Jean-Pierre Fouque (2010). Short-Maturity Asymptotics for a Fast Mean-Reverting Heston Stochastic Volatility Model. *SIAM Journal on Financial Mathematics* **1**(1): 126–41.

Fonseca, Jose Da, Martino Grasselli and Claudio Tebaldi (2008). A Multifactor Volatility Heston Model. *Quantitative Finance* **8**(6): 591–604.

Fouque, Jean-Pierre, George Papanicolaou and K. Ronnie Sircar (2000). Mean-Reverting Stochastic Volatility. *International Journal of Theoretical and Applied Finance* **3**(1): 101.

Fruhwirth-Schnatter, Sylvia and Leopold Sogner (2008). Bayesian Estimation of the Multi-Factor Heston Stochastic Volatility Model. *Communications in Dependability and Quality Management* **11**(4): 5–25.

Heston, Steven (1993). A Closed Form Solution for Options with Stochastic Volatility with Applications to Bond and Currency Options. *Review of Financial Studies* **6**(2): 327–43.

Hobson, David (2004). Stochastic Volatility Models, Correlation, and the q-Optimal Measure. *Mathematical Finance* **14**(4): 537–56.

Ito, Kiyoshi (1951). On stochastic differential equations. *Memoirs of the American Mathematical Society* **4**: 1–51.

Kahl, Christian and Peter Jackel (2006). Fast Strong Approximation Monte Carlo Schemes for Stochastic Volatility Models. *Quantitative Finance* **6**(6): 513–36.

Keynes, John Maynard (1936). *The General Theory of Employment, Interest and Money*. Macmillan, Cambridge University Press, New York.

Lee, Roger W. (2004). Implied Volatility: Statics, Dynamics, and Probabilistic Interpretation. *Recent Advances in Applied Probability*. Springer US, New York.

Lin, Guanzhi (2010). *Having a Date With Option*. Jucaizixun, Taiwan.

Luo, Xingguo and Jin Zhang (2010). The Term Structure of VIX. *2010 Financial Management Association (FMA) European Conference*. Hamburg, Germany.

Merton, Robert C., Myron S. Scholes and Mathew L. Gladstein (1978). The Return and Risk of Alternative Call-Option Portfolio Investment Strategies *The Journal of Business* **51**(2): 183–242

Merton, Robert C., Myron S. Scholes and Mathew L. Gladstein (1982). The Returns and Risks of Alternative Put-Option Portfolio Investment Strategies. *The Journal of Business* **55**(1): 1–55.

Moodley, Nimalin (2005). *The Heston Model: a Practical Approach with Matlab Code*. University of the Witwatersrand, Johannesburg.

Ncube, Moeti (2009). *Stochastic Models and Inferences for Commodity Futures Pricing*. Florida State University, Tallahassee.

Perelló, Josep, Jaume Masoliver and Napoleón Anento (2004). A Comparison between Several Correlated Stochastic Volatility Models. *Physica A: Statistical Mechanics and its Applications* **344**(1): 134–7.

Ross, Sheldon M. (2007). *Introduction to Probability Models*. Academic Press, Salt Lake City.

Ross, Stephen A. (1976). Option and Efficiency. *Quarterly Journal of Economics* **90**(1): 75–89.

Rubinstein, Mark (1994). Implied Binomial Trees. *Journal of Finance* **49**: 771–818.

Saikat, Nandi (1998). How Important is the Correlation between Returns and Volatility in a Stochastic Volatility Model? Empirical Evidence from Pricing and Hedging in the S&P 500 Index Options Market. *Journal of Banking and Finance* **22**: 589–610.

Sepp, Artur (2002). *Pricing Barrier Options under Local Volatility*. Mathematics of Computation, Raleigh, NC.

Sepp, Artur (2008). Pricing Options on Realized Variance in the Heston Model with Jumps in Returns and Volatility. *Journal of Computational Finance* **11**(4): 33–70.

Shehata, Emad Abd Elmessih and Mickaiel Sahra Khaleel (2012). IMVOL: Stata Module to Compute Implied Volatility in Black–Scholes European Option Pricing Model. Persistent link: http://EconPapers.repec.org/RePEc:boc:bocode:s457390.

Taylor, Stephen, Pradeep Yadav and Yuanyuan Zhang (2010). The Information Content of Implied Volatilities and Model-free Volatility Expectations: Evidence from Options Written on Individual Stocks. *Journal of Banking and Finance* **34**: 871–81.

Zhang, Jin and Yi Xiang (2008). The Implied Volatility Smirk. *Quantitative Finance* **8**: 263–84.

Index

at-the-money 7, 29, 34, 59–61, 71
auto-regression 51, 56

Black–Scholes model 4

call-put spread 71, 75, 81
Capital Asset Pricing Model (CAPM) 25
constant elasticity volatility (CEV) 7, 10–15, 21–4, 49, 50, 52
correlation 4–5, 7, 9, 10, 13, 14, 16–24, 51–6, 71
covariance 17
CVaR 31–3, 35, 37, 58–66, 69, 70

drift rate 9, 10, 20, 48, 54, 55

European options 2, 9
exercise price 26–8, 30, 36, 37, 72
expected return 33, 35, 59, 61, 62, 64–70
expiration date 34, 36, 37, 39, 61, 72

five-day-ahead 48, 49, 56
Fourier Transform 51

Geometrical Brownian movement (GBM) 7, 11, 13, 21, 26

Heston model 4–7, 9, 12, 14, 16–24, 51–7
HIBOR 10, 20, 48, 54
historical volatility 52, 72

implied volatility 2–13, 15, 20–3, 41, 43, 44, 47, 54–6, 71–80
in-the-money 29
input-output ratio 35, 37
interest rate 3, 10–12, 20–2, 34, 42, 46, 54, 55, 60, 62, 73
Ito's Lemma 27

least squares method 8, 19, 50
leverage 11, 21, 25, 31, 32
local volatility 4, 41–50

maturity 1–8, 11–13, 18, 23, 42–4, 46, 47, 62, 72, 73
Mean Absolute Error 14, 49
mean-reversion process 4, 41, 42, 44, 50
model-free 6–12, 14–15
Monte Carlo simulation 11, 13, 22, 33, 35, 37, 38, 42, 46, 49, 50, 60–3, 66, 67, 69, 70

nonlinear optimization 42
normal distribution 3, 10, 20, 22, 27, 46, 48, 55

one-day-ahead 14–15, 24, 48–9, 56
option strategies 32–4, 38–40, 58–68
out-of-the-money 3, 8, 29, 34, 55, 62, 71, 80

Pearson's correlation 17
polynomial regression 51, 53, 54, 56
put-call parity 36

realized variance 51, 52
realized volatility 7, 52
risk management 25–7, 29–32, 39, 58–60, 65–8
risk premium 42
rolling process 47

short-swing trading 47
simple regression 51, 53, 56, 57
Stochastic differential equation (SDE) 9–11, 20, 21, 26, 48, 54
stochastic volatility 4–6, 9, 11, 15, 16, 20–3, 42, 53–4, 73

Strike 2–4, 6–8, 11, 18, 34, 41, 44, 46, 60, 62, 71–4

term structure 3, 4, 6–15, 20–23, 41, 54, 55, 71–81
Tikhonov regularization 42
time series 12, 13, 15–18, 22, 23, 41, 52
time to maturity 2–4, 8, 11, 18, 46, 47, 62, 72, 73

VaR 26, 31–3, 35, 37–9, 58–67, 69, 70
volatility of volatility 5, 7, 10, 12, 13, 16, 21, 22, 50–2, 55

Wiener process 2, 5, 7, 10, 20, 26, 48, 52, 54, 55
Wing Fung Financial Group 29
Wishart process 51

For Product Safety Concerns and Information please contact our EU representative GPSR@taylorandfrancis.com
Taylor & Francis Verlag GmbH, Kaufingerstraße 24, 80331 München, Germany

www.ingramcontent.com/pod-product-compliance
Lightning Source LLC
LaVergne TN
LVHW021114300926
849160LV00009B/728

9781138916265